Learning Mathematics with the Abacus

Year 2

by
Sheikh Faisal Sheikh Mansor

KREATIF KEMBARA SDN. BHD.

ISBN : 983-9278-51-7
©KREATIF KEMBARA SDN. BHD.

KREATIF KEMBARA SDN. BHD.
11, 1st floor, Jalan Mewah, SS22/11, Damansara Jaya, 47400 Petaling Jaya, Selangor.
Tel : 03-77284400 / 77269431
Fax : 03-77284434
Email : admin@kreatifkembara.com
Printed by : Swan Printing Sdn. Bhd.

Contents

Unit 1 — Numbers up to 1000

 Let's say!

This is one block.

| | 1 one | |

These are ten blocks. Let's count in ones.

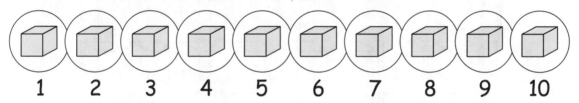

1 2 3 4 5 6 7 8 9 10

 10 ones make ten!

10 ten

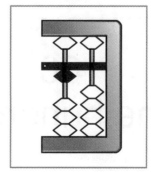

These are one hundred blocks. Let's count in tens.

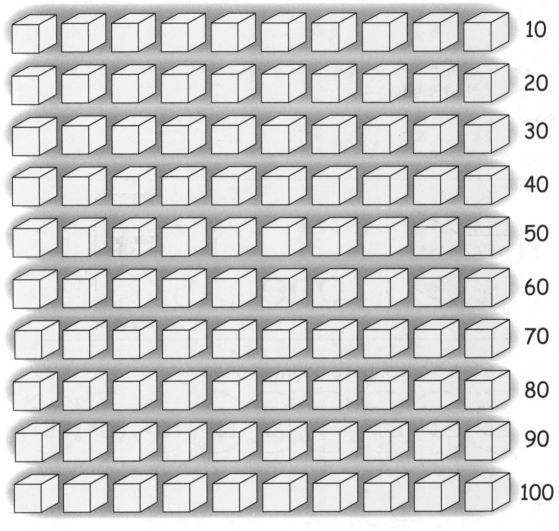

10
20
30
40
50
60
70
80
90
100

10 tens make one hundred!

100
one hundred

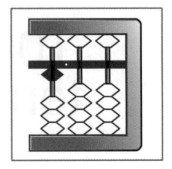

These are one thousand blocks. Let's count on in hundreds.

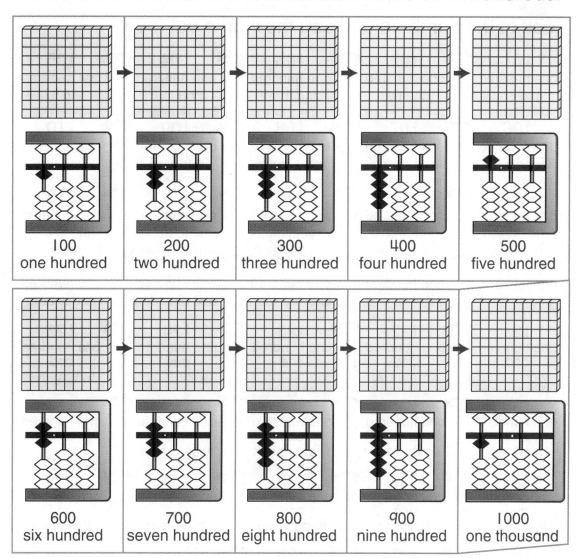

100	200	300	400	500
one hundred	two hundred	three hundred	four hundred	five hundred

600	700	800	900	1000
six hundred	seven hundred	eight hundred	nine hundred	one thousand

10 hundreds make one thousand!

1000
one thousand

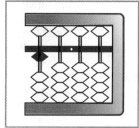

Let's count on in ones!

Look at the numbers and say the words out loud.

101 one hundred and one	102 one hundred and two	103 one hundred and three	104 one hundred and four	105 one hundred and five
106 one hundred and six	107 one hundred and seven	108 one hundred and eight	109 one hundred and nine	110 one hundred and ten
111 one hundred and eleven	112 one hundred and twelve	113 one hundred and thirteen	114 one hundred and fourteen	115 one hundred and fifteen
116 one hundred and sixteen	117 one hundred and seventeen	118 one hundred and eighteen	119 one hundred and nineteen	120 one hundred and twenty
121 one hundred and twenty-one	122 one hundred and twenty-two	123 one hundred and twenty-three	124 one hundred and twenty-four	125 one hundred and twenty-five
126 one hundred and twenty-six	127 one hundred and twenty-seven	128 one hundred and twenty-eight	129 one hundred and twenty-nine	130 one hundred and thirty
131 one hundred and thirty-one	132 one hundred and thirty-two	133 one hundred and thirty-three	134 one hundred and thirty-four	135 one hundred and thirty-five
136 one hundred and thirty-six	137 one hundred and thirty-seven	138 one hundred and thirty-eight	139 one hundred and thirty-nine	140 one hundred and forty
141 one hundred and forty-one	142 one hundred and forty-two	143 one hundred and forty-three	144 one hundred and forty-four	145 one hundred and forty-five
146 one hundred and forty-six	147 one hundred and forty-seven	148 one hundred and forty-eight	149 one hundred and forty-nine	150 one hundred and fifty

151 one hundred and fifty-one	152 one hundred and fifty-two	153 one hundred and fifty-three	154 one hundred and fifty-four	155 one hundred and fifty-five
156 one hundred and fifty-six	157 one hundred and fifty-seven	158 one hundred and fifty-eight	159 one hundred and fifty-nine	160 one hundred and sixty
161 one hundred and sixty-one	162 one hundred and sixty-two	163 one hundred and sixty-three	164 one hundred and sixty-four	165 one hundred and sixty-five
166 one hundred and sixty-six	167 one hundred and sixty-seven	168 one hundred and sixty-eight	169 one hundred and sixty-nine	170 one hundred and seventy
171 one hundred and seventy-one	172 one hundred and seventy-two	173 one hundred and seventy-three	174 one hundred and seventy-four	175 one hundred and seventy-five
176 one hundred and seventy-six	177 one hundred and seventy-seven	178 one hundred and seventy-eight	179 one hundred and seventy-nine	180 one hundred and eighty
181 one hundred and eighty-one	182 one hundred and eighty-two	183 one hundred and eighty-three	184 one hundred and eighty-four	185 one hundred and eighty-five
186 one hundred and eighty-six	187 one hundred and eighty-seven	188 one hundred and eighty-eight	189 one hundred and eighty-nine	190 one hundred and ninety
191 one hundred and ninety-one	192 one hundred and ninety-two	193 one hundred and ninety-three	194 one hundred and ninety-four	195 one hundred and ninety-five
196 one hundred and ninety-six	197 one hundred and ninety-seven	198 one hundred and ninety-eight	199 one hundred and ninety-nine	200 two hundred

How do we represent two hundred on the abacus?

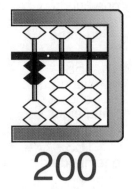

200

What number comes after two hundred?
Let's move up one on the abacus. Remember to use your thumb to move up lower beads!

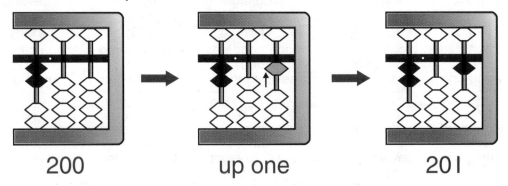

200   up one   201

Two hundred, up one, is two hundred and one.
The number after two hundred is two hundred and one!

Let's write!

201 two hundred and one

201 two hundred and one

....

What number comes after two hundred and one?
Let's move up one more bead at Ones.

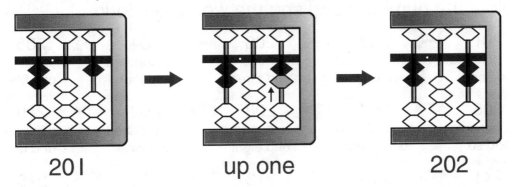

201   up one   202

Two hundred and one, up one, is two hundred and two.

The number after two hundred and one is
two hundred and two!

Let's visualise the abacus beads for 202.

Let's write!

202   two hundred and two

202 two hundred and two

. . . .

Let's continue counting on in ones!

Look at the numbers and say the words out loud.

201 two hundred and one	202 two hundred and two	203 two hundred and three	204 two hundred and four	205 two hundred and five
206 two hundred and six	207 two hundred and seven	208 two hundred and eight	209 two hundred and nine	210 two hundred and ten
211 two hundred and eleven	212 two hundred and twelve	213 two hundred and thirteen	214 two hundred and fourteen	215 two hundred and fifteen
216 two hundred and sixteen	217 two hundred and seventeen	218 two hundred and eighteen	219 two hundred and nineteen	220 two hundred and twenty
221 two hundred and twenty-one	222 two hundred and twenty-two	223 two hundred and twenty-three	224 two hundred and twenty-four	225 two hundred and twenty-five
226 two hundred and twenty-six	227 two hundred and twenty-seven	228 two hundred and twenty-eight	229 two hundred and twenty-nine	230 two hundred and thirty
231 two hundred and thirty-one	232 two hundred and thirty-two	233 two hundred and thirty-three	234 two hundred and thirty-four	235 two hundred and thirty-five
236 two hundred and thirty-six	237 two hundred and thirty-seven	238 two hundred and thirty-eight	239 two hundred and thirty-nine	240 two hundred and forty
241 two hundred and forty-one	242 two hundred and forty-two	243 two hundred and forty-three	244 two hundred and forty-four	245 two hundred and forty-five
246 two hundred and forty-six	247 two hundred and forty-seven	248 two hundred and forty-eight	249 two hundred and forty-nine	250 two hundred and fifty

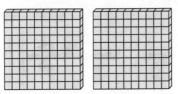

I have two hundred and fifty blocks.
I can group the blocks like this!

2 hundreds   and   5 tens

How do we represent two hundred and fifty on the abacus?
How do we move up 250?

Let's put the place values on the abacus.
Now, let's move the beads at each place value.

There are 2 Hundreds.
The digit 2 in 250 represents 200.

I Let's move up 2 at Hundreds.

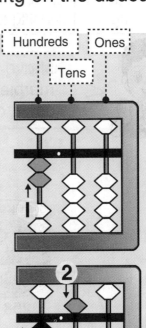

There are 5 Tens.
The digit 5 in 250 represents 50.

2 Let's move up 5 at Tens.

There are no Ones.
The digit 0 in 250 represents 0.
We do not move any beads at Ones.
We write zero as a place holder at Ones.

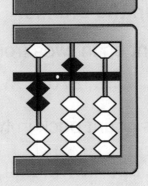

This is 250 on the abacus!

Let's count on in twos from 250!
Move the beads on the abacus according to each number as you count.

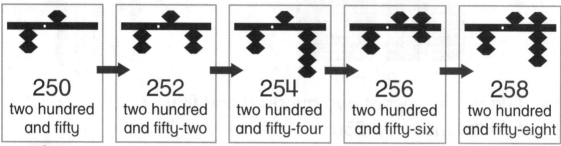

250	252	254	256	258
two hundred and fifty	two hundred and fifty-two	two hundred and fifty-four	two hundred and fifty-six	two hundred and fifty-eight

I have 258 marbles in this jar. I have more marbles on the table. I group them in twos. Let's count all my marbles.

258, 260, 262, 264, 266, 268, 270, 272

Fill in the blanks.

Count on in twos from two hundred and seventy-two.

272, ..., 276, ..., 280, ..., 284, ..., ..., 290

Let's count back in twos from two hundred and ninety.

290, 288, ..., 284, ..., ..., 278, ..., 274, ...

Let's count on in fives from 260!

Move the beads on the abacus according to each number as you count.

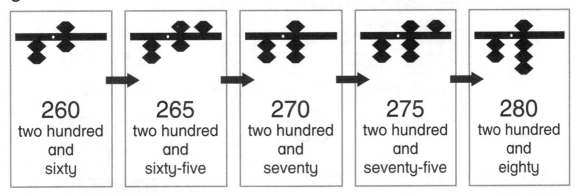

260	265	270	275	280
two hundred and sixty	two hundred and sixty-five	two hundred and seventy	two hundred and seventy-five	two hundred and eighty

Fill in the blanks as you count on in fives.

270, ..., 280, 285, ..., 295, ..., ..., ..., 315.

Let's count on in tens from 315!

Move the beads on the abacus according to each number as you count.

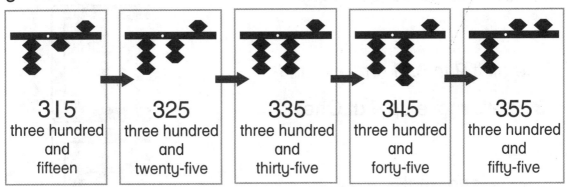

315	325	335	345	355
three hundred and fifteen	three hundred and twenty-five	three hundred and thirty-five	three hundred and forty-five	three hundred and fifty-five

Fill in the blanks as you count on in tens.

345, 355, 365, ..., 385, ..., ..., ...,425.

I have five hundred and eighty-nine blocks. I can group the blocks like this!

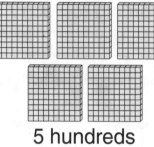

5 hundreds

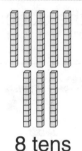

8 tens

9 ones

589

Let's put the place values on the abacus.
Now, let's move the beads at each place value.
The digit 5 in 589 represents 500.

1 Let's move up 5 at Hundreds.

The digit 8 in 589 represents 80.

2 Let's move up 8 at Tens.

The digit 9 in 589 represents 9.

3 Let's move up 9 at Ones.

This is 589 on the abacus!

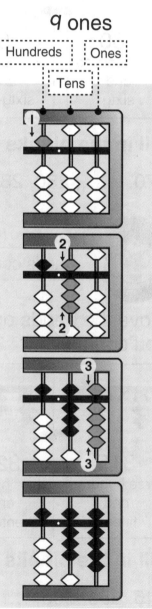

I have these rods. How many rods are there? Represent them on the abacus.

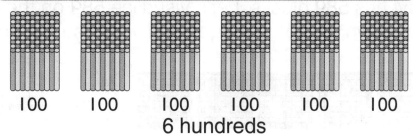

100 100 100 100 100 100

6 hundreds

5 ones

Let's represent 6 hundreds and 5 ones on the abacus.

1 First, move up 6 at Hundreds.

There are no tens. So, we use zero as a place holder. We do not move up any beads at Tens.

2 Next, let's move up 5 at Ones.

What is the number represented on this abacus? Say the number out loud and write it in the box.

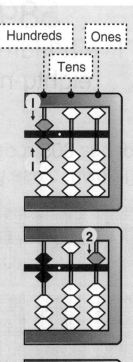

Let's visualise!

Devi has 589 blocks. Let's visualise 589 on the abacus. Lay down, close your eyes and visualise the beads.

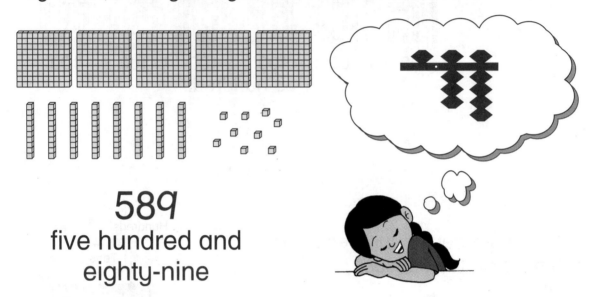

589
five hundred and eighty-nine

Andi has 605 rods. Let's visualise 605 on the abacus. Lay down, close your eyes and visualise the beads.

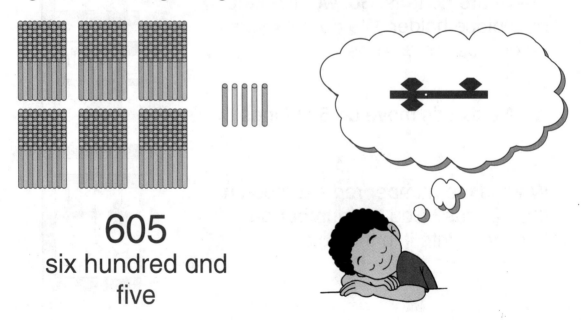

605
six hundred and five

Zura has 728 beads. Jenny has 831 beads.

Jenny has more beads than Zura.
Zura has less beads than Jenny.

831 is larger than 728
728 is smaller than 831

Which number is larger? Tick (✔) on the larger number.

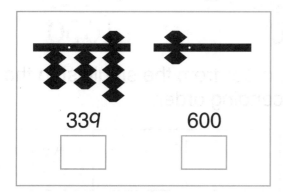

339   600

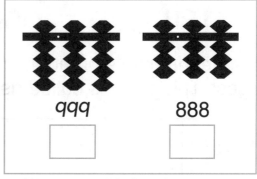

999   888

Which number is smaller? Tick (✔) on the smaller number.

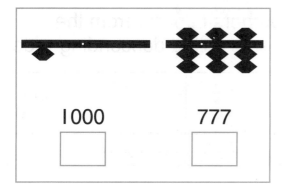

1000   777

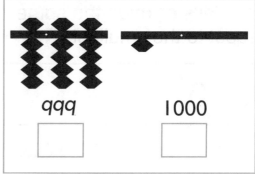

999   1000

Let's visualise the following numbers.

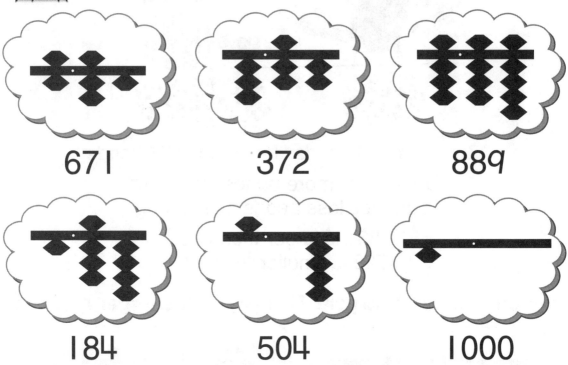

671   372   889

184   504   1000

Arrange the above numbers in order from the smallest to the largest. This order is called ascending order.

184					1000

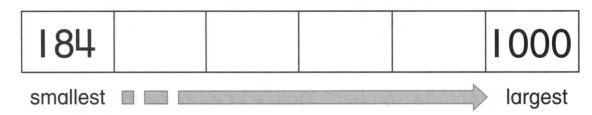

smallest ───────────────────────────→ largest

Now, let's arrange the same numbers in order from the largest to the smallest. This order is called descending order.

1000					184

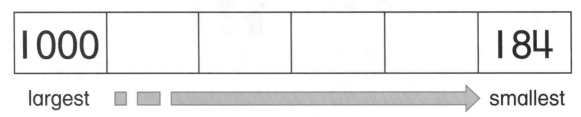

largest ───────────────────────────→ smallest

16

Let's write the missing numbers on the number line. Then, visualise the numbers on the abacus.

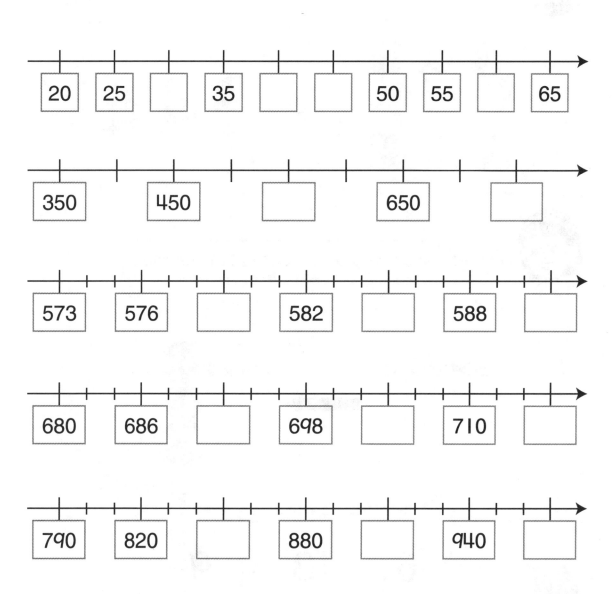

| 20 | 25 | | 35 | | | 50 | 55 | | 65 |

| 350 | | 450 | | | 650 | | |

| 573 | 576 | | 582 | | 588 | |

| 680 | 686 | | 698 | | 710 | |

| 790 | 820 | | 880 | | 940 | |

Unit 2

Addition with the highest total of 1000

How many ducks are there altogether?

 $+$

Let's visualise the beads to get the answer.

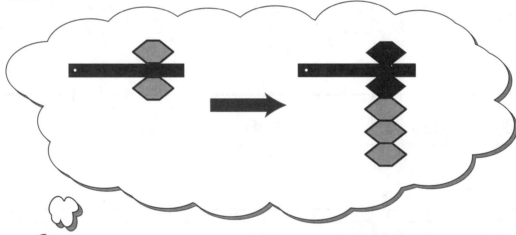

$$6 + 3 = 9$$

There are 9 ducks altogether!

Ah Wai is holding 12 straws. Devi has 6 straws.
How many straws are there altogether?

Let's visualise the beads to get the answer.

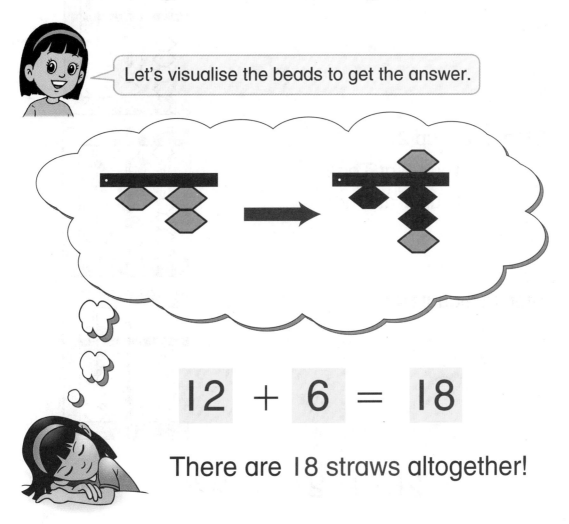

$$12 + 6 = 18$$

There are 18 straws altogether!

How do we add 26 and 21 on the abacus?

Let's try! Do you still remember the correct fingering technique to move the beads?

What is 26 + 21?

Step 1: 26, up 26

    1 up 2 at Tens

    2 up 6 at Ones

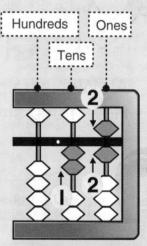

Step 2: 21, up 21

    3 up 2 at Tens

    4 up 1 at Ones

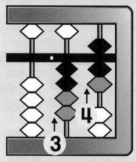

Step 3: equals 47

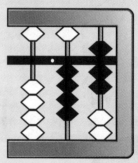

$$26 + 21 = 47$$

Jenny has 2 stamp albums. The old stamp album has 53 Malaysian stamps. The new album has only 45 Malaysian stamps. How many Malaysian stamps are there altogether?

Let's visualise this!

What is 53 + 45?

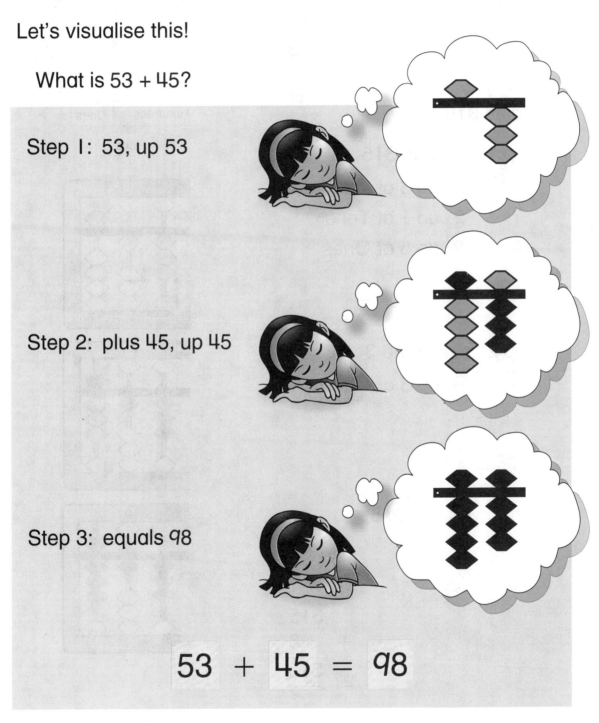

Step 1: 53, up 53

Step 2: plus 45, up 45

Step 3: equals 98

$$53 + 45 = 98$$

Below is the standard written method for addition. It reads three hundred and fifteen plus three. We write the answer in between the two horizontal lines.

$$\begin{array}{r} 315 \\ +3 \\ \hline \end{array}$$

What is $315 + 3$?

Step 1: 315, up 315

    1 up 3 at Hundreds

    2 up 1 at Tens

    3 up 5 at Ones

Step 2: plus 3, up 3

    4 up 3 at Ones

Step 3: equals 318

$$\begin{array}{r} 315 \\ +3 \\ \hline 318 \end{array}$$

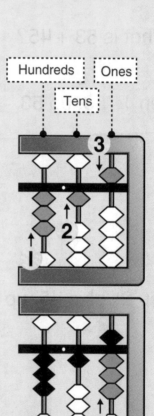

Let's add 731 and 63.

$$
\begin{array}{r}
731 \\
+ \quad 63 \\
\hline
\end{array}
$$

What is 731 + 63 ?

Step 1: 731, up 731

    1 up 7 at Hundreds

    2 up 3 at Tens

    3 up 1 at Ones

Step 2: plus 63, up 63

    4 up 6 at Tens

    5 up 3 at Ones

Step 3: equals 794

$$
\begin{array}{r}
731 \\
+ \quad 63 \\
\hline
794
\end{array}
$$

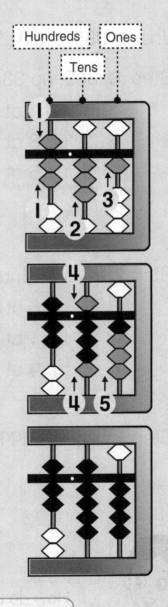

How do you write 794 in words?

Let's try 385 and 614.

$$385$$
$$+ \ 614$$
$$\overline{}$$

What is 385 + 614 ?

Step 1: 385, up 385

   1 up 3 at Hundreds

   2 up 8 at Tens

   3 up 5 at Ones

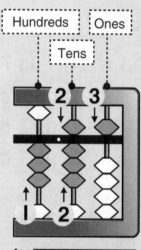

Step 2: plus 614, up 614

   4 up 6 at Hundreds

   5 up 1 at Tens

   6 up 4 at Ones

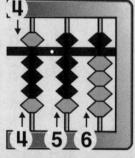

Step 3: equals 999

$$385$$
$$+ \ 614$$
$$\overline{999}$$

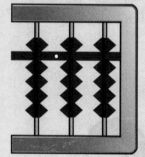

How do you write 999 in words?
Say them out loud.

Let's try adding three numbers together!

$2 + 1 + 6 = ?$

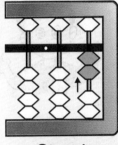

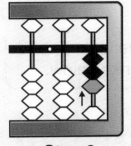

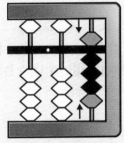

	2
	1
+	6
	9

Step 1
Up 2

Step 2
Up 1

Step 3
Up 6

$10 + 11 + 57 = ?$

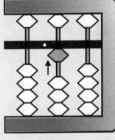

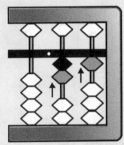

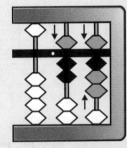

	10
	11
+	57
	78

Step 1
Up 10

Step 2
Up 11

Step 3
Up 57

$520 + 164 + 105 = ?$

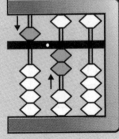

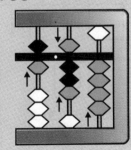

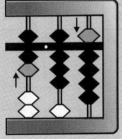

	520
	164
+	105
	789

Step 1
Up 520

Step 2
Up 164

Step 3
Up 105

In previous examples, we do not need to use the Little Friend or the Big Friend. In our next examples, we will use them in our calculation with the abacus.

Let's see if you still remember the Little Friend and the Big Friend. Fill in the blanks below.

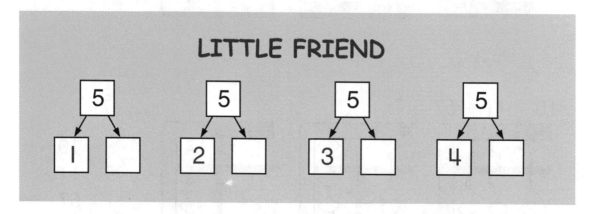

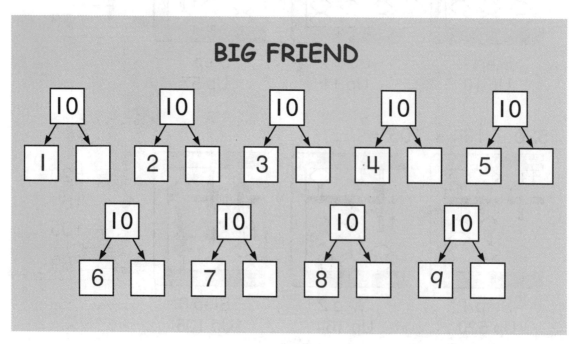

Let's try this with your abacus!

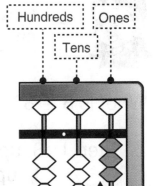

What is 3 + 4?

Step 1: 3, up 3

1 up 3 at Ones

Step 2: plus 4, up 4?

But there are not enough lower beads at Ones to up 4.
Using Little Friend of 4 (which is 1), up 4 is ...

2 up 5 at Ones and

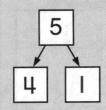

3 down 1 at Ones

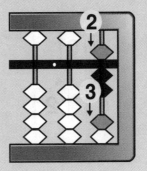

Step 3: equals 7

$$\begin{array}{r} 3 \\ + \ 4 \\ \hline 7 \end{array}$$

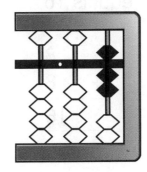

How do we add 8 and 8 on the abacus?

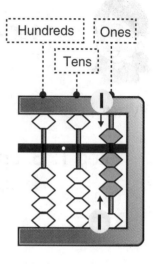

What is 8 + 8?

Step 1: 8, up 8

1 up 8 at Ones

Step 2: plus 8, up 8?

But there are not enough beads at Ones to up 8.
Using Big Friend of 8 (which is 2), up 8 is …

2 down 2 at Ones and   **3** carry 1 at Tens

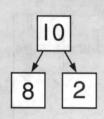

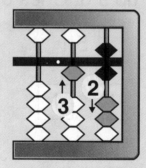

Step 3: equals 16

```
    8
+   8
─────
   16
```

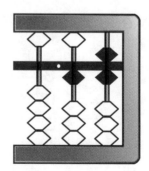

How is 8 plus 6 on the abacus?

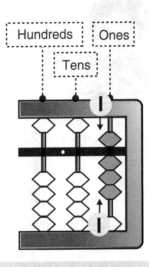

What is 8 + 6?

 Step 1: 8, up 8

  I up 8 at Ones

Step 2: plus 6, up 6?

But there are not enough beads at Ones to up 6.
Using Big Friend of 6, down 4 at Ones, carry 1 at Tens.

But there are not enough lower beads at Ones to down 4.
Using Little Friend of 4, down 4 is up 1 and down 5 at Ones.

2 up 1 at Ones, **3** down 5 at Ones, **4** carry 1 at Tens

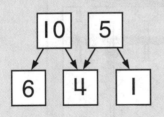

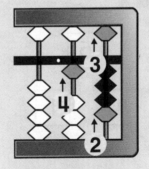

Step 3: equals 14

$$\begin{array}{r} 8 \\ +\quad 6 \\ \hline 14 \end{array}$$

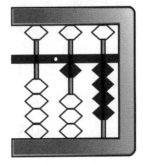

Let's add 24 and 21.

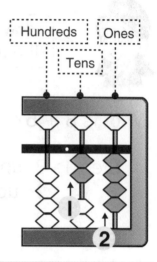

Step 1: 24, up 24

    1 up 2 at Tens

    2 up 4 at Ones

Step 2: plus 21, up 21

    3 up 2 at Tens

    up 1 at Ones?

But there are not enough lower beads at Ones to up 1.
Using Little Friend of 1 (which is 4), up 1 is ...

    4 up 5 at Ones and   **5** down 4 at Ones

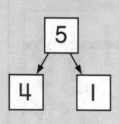

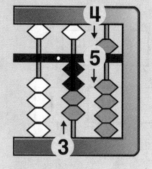

Step 3: equals 45

```
    24
 +  21
 ──────
    45
```

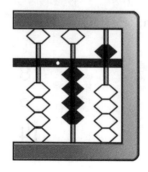

Let's add 45 and 55.

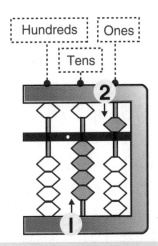

Hundreds | Ones
Tens

Step 1: 45, up 45

    1 up 4 at Tens

    2 up 5 at Ones

Step 2: plus 55, up 55

    3 up 5 at Tens

       up 5 at Ones?

But there are not enough beads at Ones to up 5.

Using Big Friend of 5 (which is 5), up 5 is ...

    4 down 5 at Ones, carry 1 at Tens?

But there are not enough beads at Tens to carry 1 (up 1).

Using Big Friend of 1 (which is 9), up 1 at Tens is ...

    5 down 9 at Tens and   **6** carry 1 at Hundreds

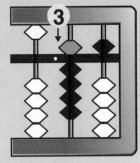

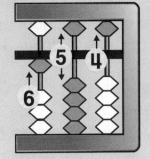

Step 3: equals 100

$$
\begin{array}{r}
45 \\
+\ \ 55 \\
\hline
100
\end{array}
$$

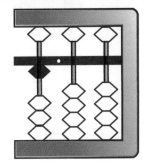

Let's add 276 and 167.

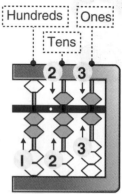

Step 1: 276, up 276

    1 up 2 at Hundreds

    2 up 7 at Tens

    3 up 6 at Ones

Step 2: plus 167, up 167

    4 up 1 at Hundreds

    up 6 at Tens?

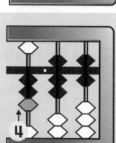

But there are not enough beads at Tens to up 6, so up 6 at Tens is down 4 at Tens and carry 1 at Hundreds.

But not enough beads at Tens, so down 4 is up 1 and down 5.

    5 up 1, down 5 at Tens

    6 carry 1 at Hundreds

    up 7 at Ones?

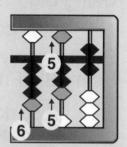

But there are not enough beads at Ones to up 7, so up 7 at Ones is down 3 at Ones and carry 1 at Tens.

But not enough beads at Ones, so down 3 is up 2 and down 5.

    7 up 2, down 5 at Ones

    8 carry 1 at Tens

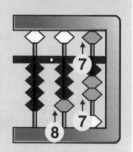

Step 3: equals 443

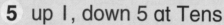

```
    276
  + 167
  -------
    443
```

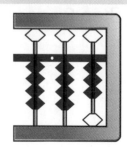

Let's add 527 and 394.

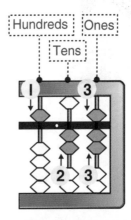

Step 1: 527, up 527

1 up 5 at Hundreds
2 up 2 at Tens
3 up 7 at Ones

Step 2: plus 394, up 394

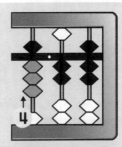

4 up 3 at Hundreds

up 9 at Tens?

But there are not enough beads at Tens to up 9, so up 9 at Tens is down 1 at Tens and carry 1 at Hundreds.

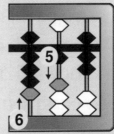

5 down 1 at Tens
6 carry 1 at Hundreds

up 4 at Ones?

But there are not enough beads at Ones to up 4, so up 4 at Ones is down 6 at Ones and carry 1 at Tens.

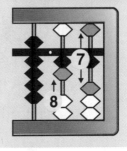

7 down 6 at Ones
8 carry 1 at Tens

Step 3: equals 921

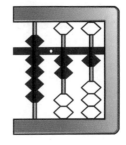

```
    527
+   394
-------
    921
```

Let's add 472 and 449.

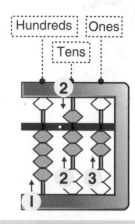

Step 1: 472, up 472

1 up 4 at Hundreds
2 up 7 at Tens
3 up 2 at Ones

Step 2: plus 449, up 449

up 4 at Hundreds
Not enough beads at Hundreds, so
4 up 5, down 1 at Hundreds

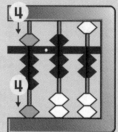

up 4 at Tens
Not enough beads at Tens, so
5 down 6 at Tens
6 carry 1 at Hundreds

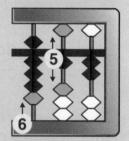

up 9 at Ones
Not enough beads at Ones, so
7 down 1 at Ones
8 carry 1 at Tens

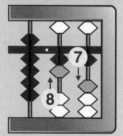

Step 3: equals 921

```
    472
 +  449
 ─────
    921
```

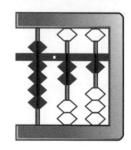

Let's visualise 283 + 657.

Visualise the beads and move your fingers as if you are moving the beads on the abacus.

Step 1: up 283

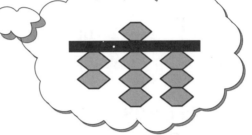

Step 2: up 657

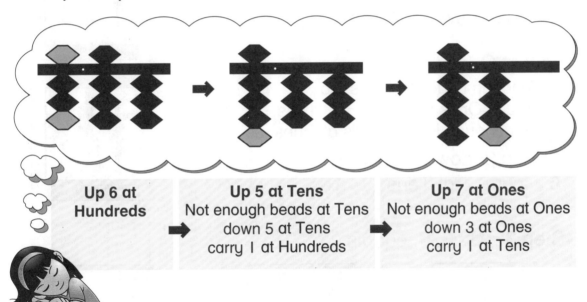

Up 6 at Hundreds	Up 5 at Tens Not enough beads at Tens down 5 at Tens carry 1 at Hundreds	Up 7 at Ones Not enough beads at Ones down 3 at Ones carry 1 at Tens

Step 3: equals 940

Let's try adding 345, 28 and 339 together on the abacus! Write the answer in the box.

```
  345
   28
+ 339
```
☐

Step 1: up 345

1 up 3 at Hundreds
2 up 4 at Tens
3 up 5 at Ones

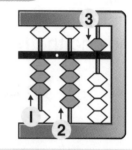

Step 2: up 28

up 2 at Tens

Not enough beads at Tens, so

4 up 5, down 3 at Tens

up 8 at Ones

Not enough beads at Ones, so
down 2 at Ones and carry 1 at Tens;
but not enough lower beads at Ones, so

5 up 3, down 5 at Ones
6 carry 1 at Tens

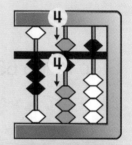

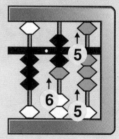

Step 3: Up 339, equals ?

 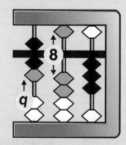 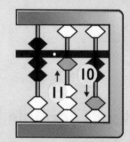

up 3 at Hundreds
Not enough beads, so

7 up 5, down 2 at Hundreds

up 3 at Tens
Not enough beads, so

8 down 7 at Tens
9 carry 1 at Hundreds

up 9 at Ones
Not enough beads, so

10 down 1 at Ones
11 carry 1 at Tens

Solve these with your abacus.

1. 9 + 7 = _____
2. 3 + 8 = _____
3. 7 + 7 = _____
4. 25 + 25 = _____
5. 34 + 13 = _____
6. 27 + 13 = _____
7. 65 + 26 = _____
8. 42 + 39 = _____
9. 44 + 43 = _____
10. 386 + 102 = _____
11. 243 + 242 = _____
12. 167 + 385 = _____
13. 444 + 333 = _____
14. 351 + 588 = _____
15. 543 + 457 = _____
16. 172 + 32 + 18 = _____
17. 231 + 25 + 34 = _____
18. 222 + 338 + 316 = _____
19. 117 + 802 + 6 = _____
20. 514 + 352 + 72 = _____

Solve these by visualising the beads and moving your fingers as if you are moving the beads on the abacus.

1. 8 + 4 = _____
2. 5 + 9 = _____
3. 6 + 7 = _____
4. 11 + 28 = _____
5. 13 + 32 = _____
6. 17 + 29 = _____
7. 52 + 20 = _____
8. 77 + 18 = _____
9. 65 + 29 = _____
10. 325 + 122 = _____
11. 264 + 152 = _____
12. 345 + 105 = _____
13. 526 + 223 = _____
14. 175 + 676 = _____
15. 474 + 247 = _____
16. 4 + 3 + 2 = _____
17. 11 + 15 + 38 = _____
18. 9 + 19 + 29 = _____
19. 214 + 428 + 20 = _____
20. 352 + 179 + 458 = _____

Unit 3

Subtraction within the range of 1000

I have 5 roses but I need 8 roses altogether. How many more roses do I need to get?

Let's visualise the beads to get the answer.

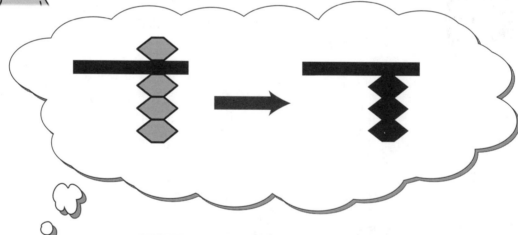

$$8 - 5 = 3$$

I need 3 more roses!

Zura has 19 apples. If she decides to give 6 apples to Ah Wai, how many more apples will she have left?

Let's visualise the beads to get the answer.

$$19 - 6 = 13$$

Zura will have 13 apples left!

How do we subtract 16 from 48 on the abacus?

Let's try!

What is 48 − 16?

Step 1: 48, up 48

    1 up 4 at Tens

    2 up 8 at Ones

Step 2: minus 16, down 16

    3 down 1 at Tens

    4 down 6 at Ones

Step 3: equals 32

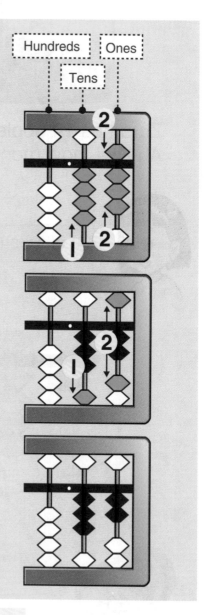

48 − 16 = 32

Some stamps are missing from Jenny's stamp album. She had 87 stamps before. Now there are only 35 stamps in the album. How many stamps are missing?

Let's visualise this!

What is 87 − 25?

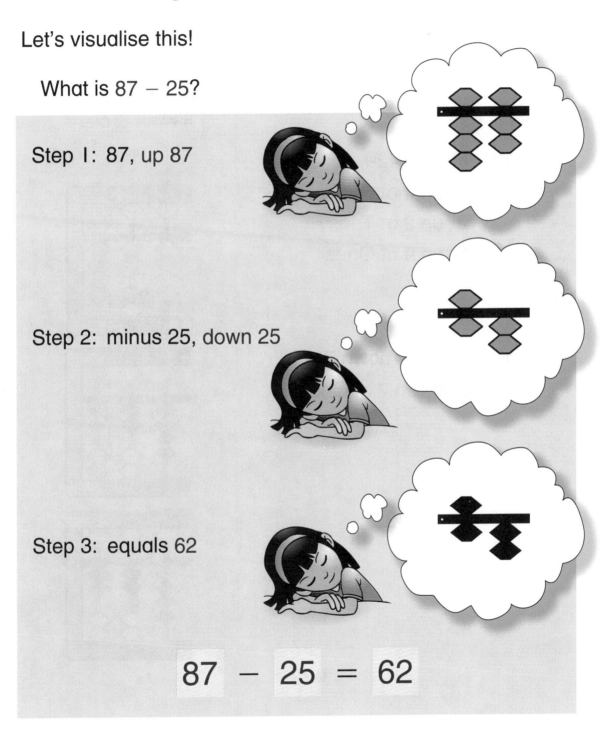

Step 1: 87, up 87

Step 2: minus 25, down 25

Step 3: equals 62

87 − 25 = 62

Just like addition, below is the standard written method for subtraction.
It reads four hundred and twenty-nine minus seven.
We write the answer in between the two horizontal lines.

$$\begin{array}{r} 429 \\ -7 \\ \hline \end{array}$$

What is 429 − 7?

Step 1: 429, up 429

1 up 4 at Hundreds

2 up 2 at Tens

3 up 9 at Ones

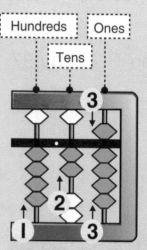

Step 2: minus 7, down 7

4 down 7 at Ones

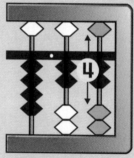

Step 3: equals 422

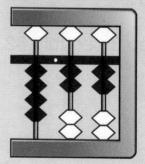

$$\begin{array}{r} 429 \\ -7 \\ \hline 422 \end{array}$$

Let's subtract 66 from 987.

$$987 - 66$$

What is 987 − 66?

Step 1: 987, up 987

    1 up 9 at Hundreds

    2 up 8 at Tens

    3 up 7 at Ones

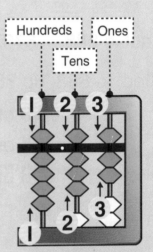

Step 2: minus 66, down 66

    4 down 6 at Tens

    5 down 6 at Ones

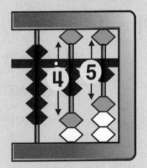

Step 3: equals 921

$$\begin{array}{r} 987 \\ -66 \\ \hline 921 \end{array}$$

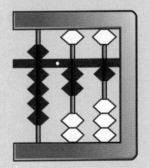

Let's try 888 minus 673.

$$888$$
$$-\ 673$$
$$\overline{}$$

What is 888 − 673?

Step 1: 888, up 888

     1 up 8 at Hundreds

     2 up 8 at Tens

     3 up 8 at Ones

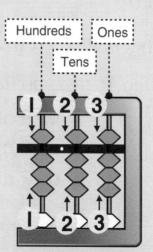

Step 2: minus 673, down 673

     4 down 6 at Hundreds

     5 down 7 at Tens

     6 down 3 at Ones

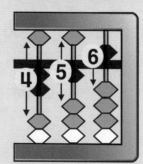

Step 3: equals 215

$$888$$
$$-\ 673$$
$$\overline{\ 215\ }$$

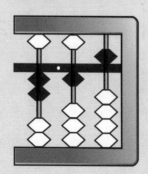

Let's try subtracting with three numbers!

$9 - 1 - 6 = ?$

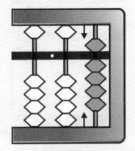 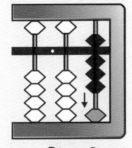 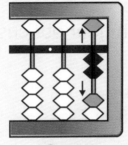 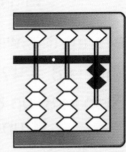

Step 1	Step 2	Step 3	Equals
Up 9	Down 1	Down 6	2

$89 - 26 - 12 = ?$

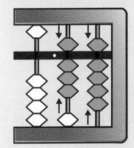 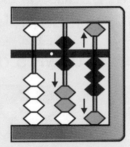 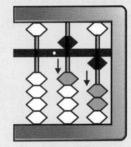 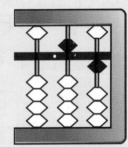

Step 1	Step 2	Step 3	Equals
Up 89	Down 26	Down 12	51

$738 - 102 - 516 = ?$

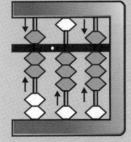 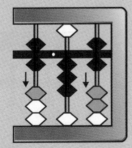 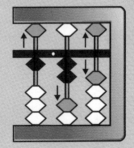 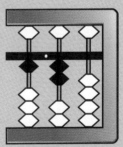

Step 1	Step 2	Step 3	Equals
Up 738	Down 102	Down 516	120

Again, in previous examples, we do not need to use the Little Friend or the Big Friend. In our next examples, we will use them in our calculation with the abacus.

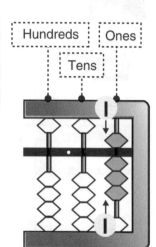

Let's try this with your abacus!

What is 8 − 4?

Step 1: 8, up 8

1 up 8 at Ones

Step 2: minus 4, down 4?

down 4 at Ones

But there are not enough lower beads at Ones to down 4. Using Little Friend of 4 (which is 1), down 4 is …

2 up 1 at Ones and

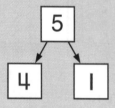

3 down 5 at Ones

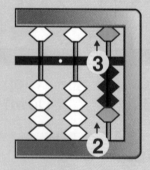

Step 3: equals 4

$$\begin{array}{r} 8 \\ -\ \ 4 \\ \hline 4 \end{array}$$

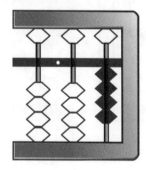

How do we subtract 8 from 17 on the abacus?

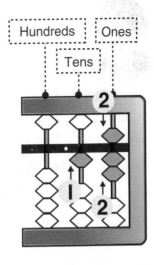

Step 1: 17, up 17

   1 up 1 at Tens

   2 up 7 at Ones

Step 2: minus 8, down 8?

But there are not enough beads at Ones to down 8.
Using Big Friend of 8 (which is 2), down 8 is …

3 remove 1 at Tens and   **4** up 2 at Ones

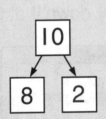

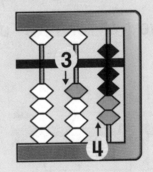

Step 3: equals 9

$$\begin{array}{r} 17 \\ -8 \\ \hline 9 \end{array}$$

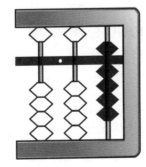

47

How is 14 minus 9 on the abacus?

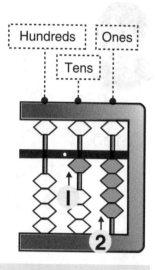

Step 1: 14, up 14

   1 up 1 at Tens

   2 up 4 at Ones

Step 2: minus 9, down 9?

But there are not enough beads at Ones to down 9.
Using Big Friend of 9, remove 1 at Tens, up 1 at Ones.

But there are not enough lower beads at Ones to up 1.
Using Little Friend of 1, up 1 is up 5 and down 4 at Ones.

3 remove 1 at Tens   **4** up 5 at Ones   **5** down 4 at Ones

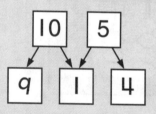

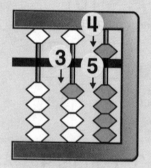

Step 3: equals 5

$$\begin{array}{r} 14 \\ -9 \\ \hline 5 \end{array}$$

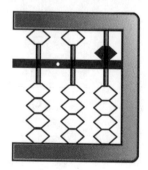

Let's subtract 17 from 41.

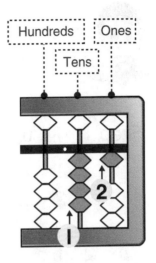

Step 1: 41, up 41

   1 up 4 at Tens

   2 up 1 at Ones

Step 2: minus 17, down 17

   3 down 1 at Tens
      down 7 at Ones?

But there are not enough lower beads at Ones to down 7.
Using Big Friend of 7 (which is 3), down 7 is ...

4 remove 1 at Tens and   **5** up 3 at Ones

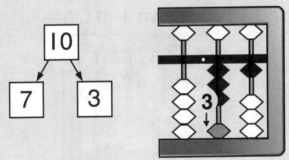

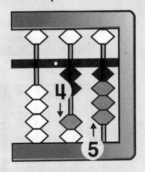

Step 3: equals 24

```
    41
 -  17
 _____
    24
```

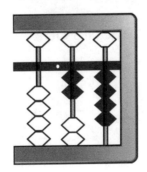

Let's do 94 minus 36.

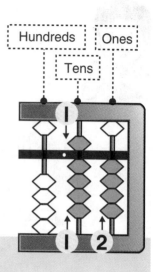

Hundreds | Tens | Ones

Step 1: 94, up 94

1 up 9 at Tens

2 up 4 at Ones

Step 2: minus 36, down 36

3 down 3 at Tens
down 6 at Ones?

But there are not enough beads at Ones to down 6.
Using Big Friend of 6 (which is 4), down 6 is ...

4 remove 1 at Tens, up 4 at Ones?

But there are not enough beads at Ones to up 4.
Using Little Friend of 4 (which is 1), up 4 at Ones is ...

5 up 5 at Ones and

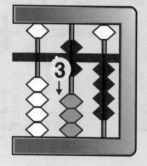

6 down 1 at Ones

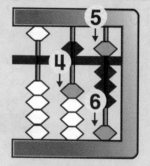

Step 3: equals 58

```
    94
 −  36
 ─────
    58
```

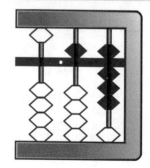

Let's take away 197 from 450.

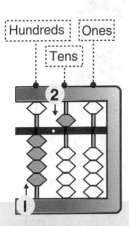

Hundreds | Tens | Ones

Step 1: 450, up 450

> **1** up 4 at Hundreds
> **2** up 5 at Tens

Step 2: minus 197, down 197

> **3** down 1 at Hundreds
>
> down 9 at Tens?

But there are not enough beads at Tens to down 9, so down 9 at Tens is remove one at Hundreds and up 1 at Tens.

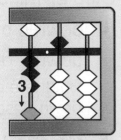

> **4** remove 1 at Hundreds
> **5** up 1 at Tens
>
> down 7 at Ones?

But there are not enough beads at Ones to down 7, so down 7 at Ones is remove 1 at Tens and up 3 at Ones.

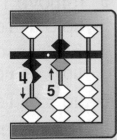

> **6** remove 1 at Tens
> **7** up 3 at Ones

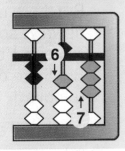

Step 3: equals 253

$$\begin{array}{r} 450 \\ -\ 197 \\ \hline 253 \end{array}$$

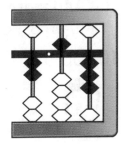

Let's remove 677 from 923.

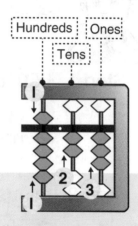

Hundreds · Ones · Tens

Step 1: 923, up 923

1 up 9 at Hundreds

2 up 2 at Tens

3 up 3 at Ones

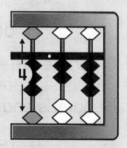

Step 2: minus 677, down 677

4 down 6 at Hundreds

down 7 at Tens?

But there are not enough beads at Tens to down 7, so down 7 at Tens is

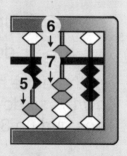

5 remove 1 at Hundreds and up 3 at Tens?

But there are not enough beads at Tens to up 3, so up 3 at Tens is

6 up 5 at Tens and **7** down 2 at Tens

down 7 at Ones?

But there are not enough beads at Ones to down 7, so down 7 at Ones is remove 1 at Tens and up 3 at Ones.

But there are not enough beads at Tens to remove 1, so down 1 at Tens is

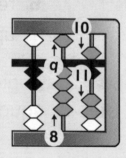

8 up 4 at Tens and **9** down 5 at Tens

And there are also not enough beads at Ones to up 3, so up 3 at Ones is

10 up 5 at Ones   **11** down 2 at Ones

What is the answer that shows on your abacus?

52

What is 1000 − 72?

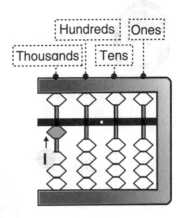

Step 1: up 1000

1 up 1 at Thousands
Zero is a place holder at Hundreds,
Tens, and Ones.

Step 2: down 72

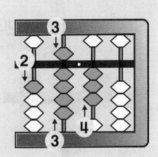

down 7 at Tens
Not enough beads at Tens, so
remove 1 at Hundreds, up 3 at Tens.
Not enough beads at Hundreds,
so remove 1 (down 1) at Hundreds is
remove 1 at Thousands, up 9 at Hundreds.

2 remove 1 at Thousands
3 up 9 at Hundreds
4 up 3 at Tens

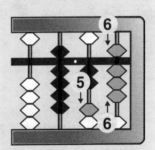

down 2 at Ones
Not enough beads at Ones, so

5 remove 1 at Tens
6 up 8 at Ones

Step 3: equals 928

```
  1000
−   72
───────
   928
```

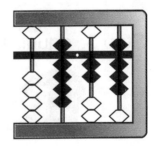

Let's visualise 737 − 248.

Visualise the beads and move your fingers as if you are moving the beads on the abacus.

Step 1: up 737

Step 2: down 248

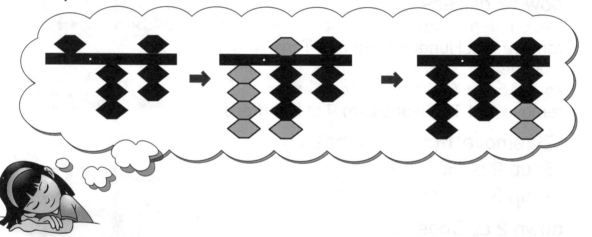

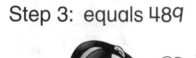

down 2 at Hundreds	down 4 at Tens Not enough beads at Tens, remove 1 at Hundreds, (not enough beads, so up 4, down 5 at Hundreds), up 6 at Tens.	down 8 at Ones Not enough beads at Ones, remove 1 at Tens, up 2 at Ones.

Step 3: equals 489

54

Let's try subtracting 236 and 487 from 952 on the abacus. Write the answer in the box.

952
− 236
− 487
☐

Step 1: up 952

1 up 9 at Hundreds

2 up 5 at Tens

3 up 2 at Ones

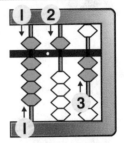

Step 2: down 236

4 down 2 at Hundreds

down 3 at Tens
Not enough beads at Tens, so

5 up 2 and   **6** down 5 at Tens

down 6 at Ones
Not enough beads at Ones, so

7 remove 1 at Tens and
up 4 at Ones but not enough beads, so

8 up 5 and   **9** down 1 at Ones

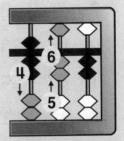

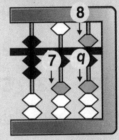

Step 3: down 487, equals ?

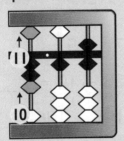

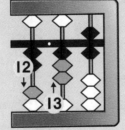

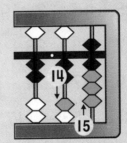

down 4 at Hundreds
Not enough beads, so

10 up 1 and

11 down 5 at Hundreds

down 8 at Tens
Not enough beads, so

12 remove 1 at Hundreds

13 up 2 at Tens

down 7 at Ones
Not enough beads, so

14 remove 1 at Tens

15 up 3 at Ones

Solve these with your abacus.

1. 7 − 3 = ___

2. 8 − 4 = ___

3. 6 − 2 = ___

4. 12 − 9 = ___

5. 14 − 7 = ___

6. 18 − 9 = ___

7. 34 − 18 = ___

8. 36 − 17 = ___

9. 45 − 23 = ___

10. 81 − 38 = ___

11. 67 − 29 = ___

12. 64 − 37 = ___

13. 100 − 1 = ___

14. 100 − 37 = ___

15. 100 − 99 = ___

16. 379 − 244 = ___

17. 408 − 256 = ___

18. 500 − 135 = ___

19. 763 − 576 = ___

20. 801 − 415 = ___

21. 838 − 464 = ___

22. 9 − 4 − 3 = ___

23. 6 − 2 − 3 = ___

24. 8 − 1 − 4 = ___

25. 15 − 3 − 9 = ___

26. 19 − 6 − 5 = ___

27. 46 − 23 − 17 = ___

28. 50 − 27 − 15 = ___

29. 87 − 19 − 54 = ___

30. 100 − 23 − 19 = ___

31. 453 − 117 − 195 = ___

32. 500 − 196 − 196 = ___

33. 777 − 399 − 199 = ___

34. 987 − 789 − 89 = ___

35. 1000 − 199 − 395 = ___

Solve these by visualising the beads and moving your fingers as if you are moving the beads on the abacus.

1. $6 - 3 =$ ___

2. $8 - 5 =$ ___

3. $6 - 1 =$ ___

4. $15 - 9 =$ ___

5. $16 - 9 =$ ___

6. $17 - 9 =$ ___

7. $31 - 10 =$ ___

8. $33 - 22 =$ ___

9. $47 - 35 =$ ___

10. $82 - 36 =$ ___

11. $97 - 39 =$ ___

12. $85 - 27 =$ ___

13. $100 - 15 =$ ___

14. $100 - 23 =$ ___

15. $100 - 50 =$ ___

16. $334 - 203 =$ ___

17. $468 - 246 =$ ___

18. $499 - 153 =$ ___

19. $715 - 478 =$ ___

20. $811 - 123 =$ ___

21. $855 - 633 =$ ___

22. $9 - 1 - 3 =$ ___

23. $8 - 2 - 6 =$ ___

24. $9 - 3 - 5 =$ ___

25. $16 - 13 - 2 =$ ___

26. $11 - 5 - 3 =$ ___

27. $45 - 15 - 23 =$ ___

28. $50 - 30 - 12 =$ ___

29. $97 - 26 - 62 =$ ___

30. $100 - 25 - 37 =$ ___

31. $485 - 171 - 232 =$ ___

32. $500 - 111 - 228 =$ ___

33. $790 - 205 - 123 =$ ___

34. $999 - 222 - 588 =$ ___

35. $1000 - 355 - 511 =$ ___

 **Unit 4** Combination of addition and subtraction within 1000

One morning, Jenny goes to the market to buy some eggs. She buys 38 eggs altogether. On the way home, she accidentally falls and breaks 15 of the eggs. She throws the broken eggs away. She goes back to the market and buys 21 more eggs. How many eggs does she have now?

 Let's try this on the abacus.

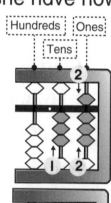

1 Jenny has 38 eggs. So, up 38
   1 up 3 at Tens
   2 up 8 at Ones

2 She breaks and throws away 15 eggs. So, down 15
   3 down 1 at Tens
   4 down 5 at Ones

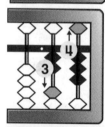

3 She buys 21 more eggs. So, up 21
   5 up 2 at Tens
   6 up 1 at Ones

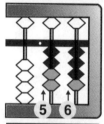

4 Equals 44
So, she has 44 eggs.

We can write the number sentence as:

$$38 - 15 + 21 = 44$$

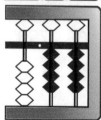

Andi has 388 Malaysian stamps in his stamp album. He gives Devi 26 Malaysian stamps in exchange for 26 Australian stamps. Andi then gives 112 American stamps to Jenny in exchange for 112 new Malaysian stamps. How many Malaysian stamps does Andi have now?

 Let's try this on the abacus.

1 Andi has 388 Malaysian stamps.
   So, up 388
   1 up 3 at Hundreds
   2 up 8 at Tens
   3 up 8 at Ones

2 He gives 26 Malaysian stamps to Devi.
   So, down 26
   4 down 2 at Tens
   5 down 6 at Ones

3 He gets 112 Malaysian stamps from Jenny.
   So, up 112
   6 up 1 at Hundreds
   7 up 1 at Tens
   8 up 2 at Ones

4 Equals 474
   So, he has 474 Malaysian stamps.

We can write the number sentence as:

$$388 - 26 + 112 = 474$$

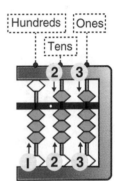

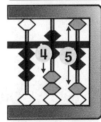

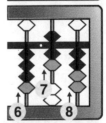

Let's visualise 33 − 21 + 27.

What is 33 − 21 + 27?

Step 1: 33, up 33

Step 2: minus 21, down 21

Step 2: plus 27, up 27

Step 4: equals 39

$$33 - 21 + 27 = 39$$

Let's visualise 58 + 31 − 66.

What is 58 + 31 − 66?

Step 1: 58, up 58

Step 2: plus 31, up 31

Step 2: minus 66, down 66

Step 4: equals 23

58 + 31 − 66 = 23

Let's visualise 208 + 70 − 155.

What is 208 + 70 − 155?

Step 1: 208, up 208

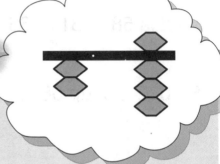

Step 2: plus 70, up 70

Step 2: minus 155, down 155

Step 4: equals 123

$$208 + 70 - 155 = 123$$

Let's visualise 639 − 527 + 776.

What is 639 − 527 + 776?

Step 1: 639, up 639

Step 2: minus 527, down 527

Step 2: plus 776, up 776

Step 4: equals 888

639 − 527 + 776 = 888

Let's visualise $910 + 38 - 406$.

What is $910 + 38 - 406$?

Step 1: 910, up 910

Step 2: plus 38, up 38

Step 2: minus 406, down 406

Step 4: equals 542

$$910 + 38 - 406 = 542$$

What is 5 − 2 + 3?

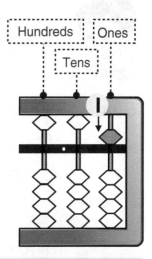

Step 1: 5, up 5

    1 up 5 at Ones

Step 2: minus 2, down 2

But there are not enough beads, so down 2 is

    2 up 3 at Ones and

    3 down 5 at Ones

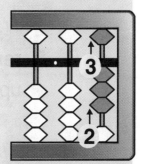

Step 3: plus 3, up 3

But there are not enough beads, so up 3 is

    4 up 5 at Ones and

    5 down 2 at Ones

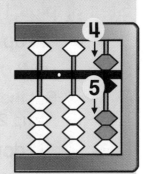

Step 4: equals 6

$$\begin{array}{r} 5 \\ -2 \\ 3 \\ \hline 6 \\ \hline \end{array}$$

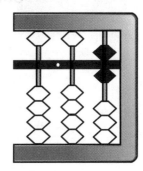

What is $18 - 9 + 12$?

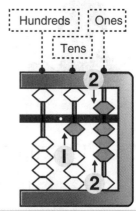

Hundreds | Tens | Ones

Step 1: 18, up 18

    1 up 1 at Tens

    2 up 8 at Ones

Step 2: minus 9, down 9

But there are not enough beads, so down 9 is

    3 remove 1 at Tens and

    4 up 1 at Ones

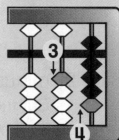

Step 3: plus 12, up 12

    5 up 1 at Tens

up 2 at Ones

But there are not enough beads, so up 2 is

    6 down 8 at Ones

    7 carry 1 at Tens

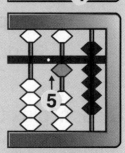

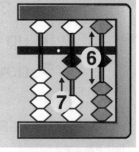

Step 4: equals 21

```
   18
 −  9
   12
 ----
   21
```

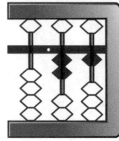

66

What is 4 + 76 − 42?

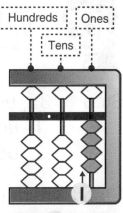

Step 1: 4, up 4

1 up 4 at Ones

Step 2: plus 76, up 76

2 up 7 at Tens

up 6 at Ones
But there are not enough beads,
so up 6 is

3 down 4 at Ones and

4 carry 1 at Tens

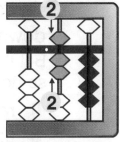

Step 3: minus 42, down 42
down 4 at Tens
But there are not enough beads,
so down 4 is

5 up 1 at Tens and

6 down 5 at Tens

down 2 at Ones
But there are not enough beads,
so down 2 is

7 remove 1 at Tens and

8 up 8 at Ones

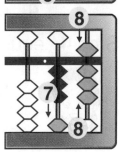

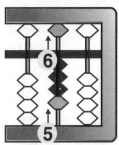

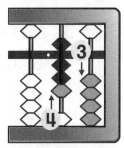

Step 4: equals?

What is your answer
on the abacus?

What is 35 − 27 + 93?

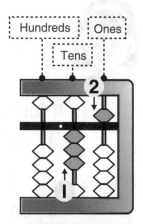

Step 1: 35, up 35

1 up 3 at Tens

2 up 5 at Ones

Step 2: minus 27, down 27

3 down 2 at Tens

down 7 at Ones

But there are not enough beads, so down 7 is

4 remove 1 at Tens and

5 up 3 at Ones

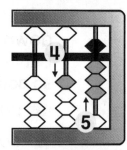

Step 3: plus 93, up 93

6 up 9 at Tens

up 3 at Ones

But there are not enough beads, so up 3 is

7 down 7 at Ones and

carry 1 at Tens

But there are not enough beads, so carry 1 (up 1) at Tens is

8 down 9 at Tens and

9 carry 1 at Hundreds

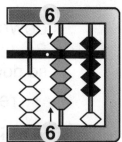

Step 4: equals?

What is your answer on the abacus?

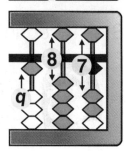

68

What is 165 − 23 + 485?

Step 1: 165, up 165

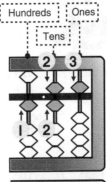

  1 up 1 at Hundreds

  2 up 6 at Tens

  3 up 5 at Ones

Step 2: minus 23, down 23

down 2 at Tens

But there are not enough beads, so down 2 is

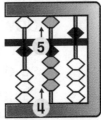

  4 up 3 at Tens and

  5 down 5 at Tens

down 3 at Ones

But there are not enough beads, so down 3 is

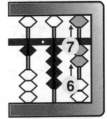

  6 up 2 at Ones and

  7 down 5 at Ones

Step 3: plus 485, up 485

up 4 at Hundreds

But there are not enough beads, so up 4 is

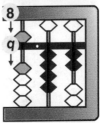

  8 up 5 at Hundreds and

  9 down 1 at Hundreds

up 8 at Tens

But there are not enough beads, so up 8 is

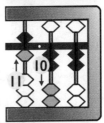

  10 down 2 at Tens and

  11 carry 1 at Hundreds

  12 up 5 at Ones

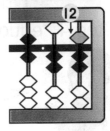

Step 4: equals?

What is 501 − 333 + 621?

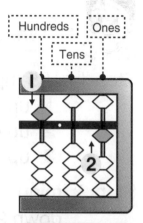

Step 1: 501, up 501

    1 up 5 at Hundreds

    2 up 1 at Ones

    Zero is a place holder at Tens

Step 2: minus 333, down 333

down 3 at Hundreds

But there are not enough beads,
so down 3 is

    3 up 2 at Hundreds and

    4 down 5 at Hundreds

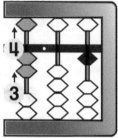

down 3 at Tens
But there are not enough beads,
so down 3 is

    5 remove 1 at Hundreds and

    6 up 7 at Tens

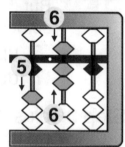

down 3 at Ones
But there are not enough beads,
so down 3 is

    7 remove 1 at Tens and

    8 up 7 at Ones

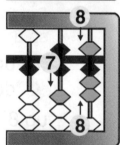

Step 3: plus 621, up 621

    9 up 6 at Hundreds

    10 up 2 at Tens

    11 up 1 at Ones

Step 4: equals?

What is your answer
on the abacus?

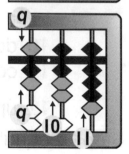

70

What is 1000 − 999 + 9?

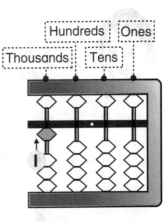

Thousands | Hundreds | Ones | Tens

Step 1: 1000, up 1000

    1 up 1 at Thousands

    Zero is a place holder at Hundreds, Tens and Ones

Step 2: minus 999, down 999

    down 9 at Hundreds

    But there are not enough beads, so down 9 is

    2 remove 1 at Thousands and

    3 up 1 at Hundreds

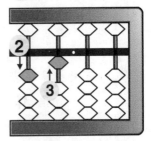

    down 9 at Tens

    But there are not enough beads, so down 9 is

    4 remove 1 at Hundreds and

    5 up 1 at Tens

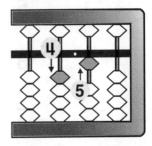

    down 9 at Ones

    But there are not enough beads, so down 9 is

    6 remove 1 at Tens and

    7 up 1 at Ones

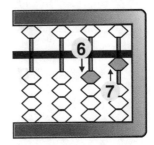

Step 3: plus 9, up 9

    up 9 at Ones

    But there are not enough beads, so up 9 is

    8 down 1 at Ones and

    9 carry 1 at Tens

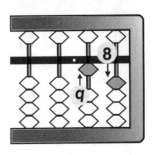

Step 4: equals?

Let's try these with your abacus.
Write your answers in the boxes accordingly.

1 999 + 1 − 385 = ☐

2 825 − 285 + 109 = ☐

3 105 − 98 + 823 = ☐

4 703 + 255 − 349 = ☐

5 333 − 244 + 556 = ☐

6 201 − 99 + 693 = ☐

7 881 + 89 − 97 = ☐

8 134 + 521 − 228 = ☐

9 500 − 300 + 800 = ☐

10 401 − 95 + 578 = ☐

11 666 − 333 + 222 = ☐

12 514 + 196 − 299 = ☐

Visualise the bead movements to solve these. Move your fingers as you would move the beads on the abacus.

1. $999 - 385 + 1$ = ☐

2. $825 - 205 + 374$ = ☐

3. $787 - 36 + 223$ = ☐

4. $664 + 335 - 999$ = ☐

5. $589 - 221 + 611$ = ☐

6. $444 - 121 + 291$ = ☐

7. $331 + 88 - 103$ = ☐

8. $222 + 539 - 350$ = ☐

9. $123 + 345 - 209$ = ☐

10. $927 - 315 + 198$ = ☐

11. $700 - 287 + 500$ = ☐

12. $1000 - 888 + 559$ = ☐

Let's look at the standard written method for writing a combination of addition and subtraction in a number sentence.

268 + 386 − 289 = ?

```
    2 6 8
    3 8 6
 −  2 8 9
 _____

 _____
```

Use your abacus to calculate and write the answer above.

129 − 47 + 731 = ?

```
    1 2 9
 −    4 7
    7 3 1
 _____

 _____
```

Use your abacus to calculate and write the answer above.

83 − 9 + 550 = ?

```
       8 3
 −       9
    5 5 0
 _____

 _____
```

Use your abacus to calculate and write the answer above.

491 − 200 + 39 = ?

```
    4 9 1
 −  2 0 0
       3 9
 _____

 _____
```

Use your abacus to calculate and write the answer above.

```
    444              20            113
  - 193             615          -  57
    601           - 189              8
  _____         _____        _____

  _____         _____        _____

    927              73            254
  - 564              21            660
    483           -  89          - 362
  _____         _____        _____

  _____         _____        _____
```

Now, let's solve these mentally. Move your fingers accordingly as you visualise the bead movements.

```
     24              74             84
  -   6            - 18           - 29
      9              25             62
  _____         _____        _____

  _____         _____        _____

    264             721            841
  -  57           - 217          - 286
    437             172            445
  _____         _____        _____

  _____         _____        _____
```

Devi, Andi, Jenny and Ah Wai are each holding a number card. Let's try to fill in the boxes below with these numbers so that the number sentence is true.

$$\boxed{} - \boxed{} + \boxed{} = \boxed{}$$

Compare your answer with your friends. Do they get the same answer as you? Can you rearrange these numbers and still get a true answer?

How would you rearrange these numbers so that the number sentences are true? Fill in the boxes with the right numbers accordingly.

9   81   19   71

☐ – ☐ + ☐ = ☐

413   37   375   75

☐ – ☐ + ☐ = ☐

629   756   197   324

☐ – ☐ + ☐ = ☐

Multiplication of basic facts within 2, 3, 4 and 5 times-tables

There are 3 bicycles here. Each bicycle has 2 wheels. How many wheels are there altogether? Let's count them.

There are 6 wheels altogether!

Let's look at it again. Bicycle 1 has 2 wheels. Bicycle 2 has 2 wheels. Bicycle 3 has 2 wheels. So,

$$2 + 2 + 2 = 6$$

We can also write the above sentence this way:

$$3 \times 2 = 6$$

Since there are 3 bicycles and each bicycle has 2 wheels. The total number of wheels is 6.

Let's say!

3	×	2	=	6
three	times	two	equals	six
three	multiplied by	two	is equal to	six

There are 6 plates here. On each plate, there are 3 oranges. How many oranges are there altogether? Let's count them.

There are 18 oranges altogether!

Let's look at it again. There are 6 plates. Each plate has 3 oranges. So, total number of oranges is

$$3 + 3 + 3 + 3 + 3 + 3 = 18$$

We can also write the above sentence this way:

$$6 \times 3 = 18$$

Let's say!

six times three equals eighteen

six multiplied by three is equal to eighteen

Multiplication is repeated addition!

Here are some apples packed in boxes. There are 7 boxes. Each box has 2 apples. How many apples are there altogether?

Let's count the total number of apples in ones.

1, 2, 3, 4, 5, 6, 7, 8, 9, 10, 11, 12, 13, 14

There are 14 apples altogether.

We can also count the apples in twos.

2, 4, 6, 8, 10, 12, 14

We can add all the apples in the boxes.

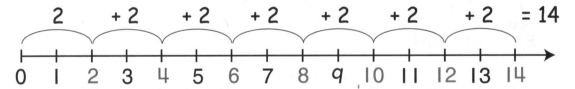

We can also do a multiplication instead of a repeat addition. Since there are 7 boxes and each box has 2 apples, the total number of apples is

$$7 \times 2 = 14$$
seven times two equals fourteen

80

Look at my toy cars. I have 3 cars. Each car has 4 wheels. How many wheels are there altogether?

Let's do skip counting and count in fours.

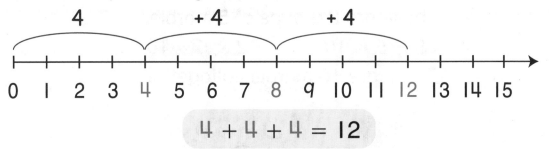

$$4 + 4 + 4 = 12$$

There are 12 wheels altogether.

Let's do a multiplication to find the answer.

How many toy cars are there? **3**

How many wheels are there on each car? **4**

So, the total number of wheels is

3 × **4** = ☐

There are 5 marbles in each group. How many marbles are there altogether? Let's count the marbles in fives.

This is 1 group of 5 marbles. There are 5 marbles altogether.

$$1 \times 5 = 5$$

5   10

These are 2 groups of 5 marbles.

$$5 + 5 = 10 \qquad 2 \times 5 = 10$$

There are 10 marbles altogether.

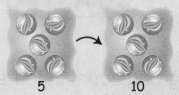

5   10   15

These are 3 groups of 5 marbles

$$5 + 5 + 5 = 15 \qquad 3 \times 5 = 15$$

There are 15 marbles altogether.

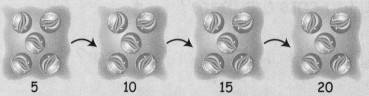

5   10   15   20

These are 4 groups of 5 marbles

$$5 + 5 + 5 + 5 = 20 \qquad 4 \times 5 = 20$$

There are 20 marbles altogether.

Let's complete this table!

	1 group of 5 Count in fives: 5	$1 \times 5 = 5$
	2 groups of 5 Count in fives: 5, 10	$5 + 5 = 10$ $2 \times 5 = 10$
	3 groups of 5 Count in fives: 5, 10, 15	$5 + 5 + 5 = 15$ $3 \times 5 = 15$
	4 groups of 5 Count in fives: 5, 10, 15, 20	$5 + 5 + 5 + 5 = 20$ $4 \times 5 = 20$
	5 groups of 5 Count in fives: 5, 10, 15, 20, ____	$5 \times 5 = $ ____
	6 groups of 5 Count in fives: 5, 10, 15, 20, ____, ____	$6 \times 5 = $ ____
	7 groups of 5 Count in fives: 5, 10, 15, 20, ____, ____, ____	$7 \times 5 = $ ____
	8 groups of 5 Count in fives: 5, 10, 15, 20, ____, ____ ____, ____	$8 \times 5 = $ ____
	9 groups of 5 Count in fives: 5, 10, 15, 20, ____, ____ ____, ____, ____	$9 \times 5 = $ ____

83

Let's complete this table!

	1 group of 4 Count in fours: 4	$1 \times 4 = 4$
	2 groups of 4 Count in fours: 4, 8	$4 + 4 = 8$ $2 \times 4 = 8$
	3 groups of 4 Count in fours: 4, 8, 12	$4 + 4 + 4 = 12$ $3 \times 4 = 12$
	4 groups of 4 Count in fours: 4, 8, 12, 16	$4 + 4 + 4 + 4 = 16$ $4 \times 4 = 16$
	5 groups of 4 Count in fours: 4, 8, 12, 16, ___	$5 \times 4 =$ ___
	6 groups of 4 Count in fours: 4, 8, 12, 16, ___, ___	$6 \times 4 =$ ___
	7 groups of 4 Count in fours: 4, 8, 12, 16, ___, ___, ___	$7 \times 4 =$ ___
	8 groups of 4 Count in fours: 4, 8, 12, 16, ___, ___ ___, ___	$8 \times 4 =$ ___
	9 groups of 4 Count in fours: 4, 8, 12, 16, ___, ___ ___, ___, ___	$9 \times 4 =$ ___

Let's complete this table!

	1 group of 3 Count in threes: 3	$1 \times 3 = 3$
	2 groups of 3 Count in threes: 3, 6	$3 + 3 = 6$ $2 \times 3 = 6$
	3 groups of 3 Count in threes: 3, 6, 9	$3 + 3 + 3 = 9$ $3 \times 3 = 9$
	4 groups of 3 Count in threes: 3, 6, 9, 12	$3 + 3 + 3 + 3 = 12$ $4 \times 3 = 12$
	5 groups of 3 Count in threes: 3, 6, 9, 12, ____	$5 \times 3 = $ ___
	6 groups of 3 Count in threes: 3, 6, 9, 12, ____, ____	$6 \times 3 = $ ___
	7 groups of 3 Count in threes: 3, 6, 9, 12, ____, ____, ____	$7 \times 3 = $ ___
	8 groups of 3 Count in threes: 3, 6, 9, 12, ____, ____ ____, ____	$8 \times 3 = $ ___
	9 groups of 3 Count in threes: 3, 6, 9, 12, ____, ____ ____, ____, ____	$9 \times 3 = $ ___

Let's complete this table!

●●	1 group of 2 Count in twos: 2	$1 \times 2 = 2$
●● ●●	2 groups of 2 Count in twos: 2, 4	$2 + 2 = 4$ $2 \times 2 = 4$
●● ●● ●●	3 groups of 2 Count in twos: 2, 4, 6	$2 + 2 + 2 = 6$ $3 \times 2 = 6$
●● ●● ●● ●●	4 groups of 2 Count in twos: 2, 4, 6, 8	$2 + 2 + 2 + 2 = 8$ $4 \times 2 = 8$
●● ●● ●● ●● ●●	5 groups of 2 Count in twos: 2, 4, 6, 8, ___	$5 \times 2 = $ ___
●● ●● ●● ●● ●● ●●	6 groups of 2 Count in twos: 2, 4, 6, 8, ___, ___	$6 \times 2 = $ ___
●● ●● ●● ●● ●● ●● ●●	7 groups of 2 Count in twos: 2, 4, 6, 8, ___, ___, ___	$7 \times 2 = $ ___
●● ●● ●● ●● ●● ●● ●● ●●	8 groups of 2 Count in twos: 2, 4, 6, 8, ___, ___ ___, ___	$8 \times 2 = $ ___
●● ●● ●● ●● ●● ●● ●● ●● ●● ●●	9 groups of 2 Count in twos: 2, 4, 6, 8, ___, ___ ___, ___, ___	$9 \times 2 = $ ___

Let's recall and complete these times-tables.

2 Times-table

$1 \times 2 = \underline{}$
$2 \times 2 = \underline{}$
$3 \times 2 = \underline{}$
$4 \times 2 = \underline{}$
$5 \times 2 = \underline{}$
$6 \times 2 = \underline{}$
$7 \times 2 = \underline{}$
$8 \times 2 = \underline{}$
$9 \times 2 = \underline{}$

3 Times-table

$1 \times 3 = \underline{}$
$2 \times 3 = \underline{}$
$3 \times 3 = \underline{}$
$4 \times 3 = \underline{}$
$5 \times 3 = \underline{}$
$6 \times 3 = \underline{}$
$7 \times 3 = \underline{}$
$8 \times 3 = \underline{}$
$9 \times 3 = \underline{}$

4 Times-table

$1 \times 4 = \underline{}$
$2 \times 4 = \underline{}$
$3 \times 4 = \underline{}$
$4 \times 4 = \underline{}$
$5 \times 4 = \underline{}$
$6 \times 4 = \underline{}$
$7 \times 4 = \underline{}$
$8 \times 4 = \underline{}$
$9 \times 4 = \underline{}$

5 Times-table

$1 \times 5 = \underline{}$
$2 \times 5 = \underline{}$
$3 \times 5 = \underline{}$
$4 \times 5 = \underline{}$
$5 \times 5 = \underline{}$
$6 \times 5 = \underline{}$
$7 \times 5 = \underline{}$
$8 \times 5 = \underline{}$
$9 \times 5 = \underline{}$

You must know these multiplication tables by heart!

How do we multiply on the abacus?

We only use the abacus to multiply bigger numbers. At this point, we could not use the abacus to perform multiplications. We can only display the product of the multiplication on the abacus.

What is the product?

Let's look at the following example.

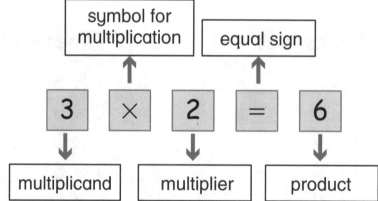

symbol for multiplication

equal sign

3 × 2 = 6

multiplicand

multiplier

product

From the above sentence, 3 is called the multiplicand. 2 is called the multiplier. 6 is called the product.

The multiplicand times the multilplier equals the product.

Yes!

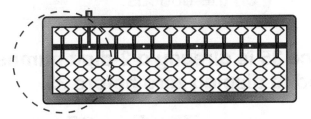

To display the product on the abacus, we need to start from the first rod on the left side of the abacus.

We also need to read the product in 2 digits.

$$3 \times 2 = 6$$

Since 6 is only 1 digit, we need to display zero before 6.

$$3 \times 2 = 06$$

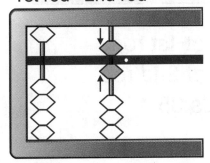

Step 1: Display 0 at 1st rod
Step 2: Up 6 at 2nd rod
Step 3: Equals 6

We must know the times-tables by heart so that we know what to display on the abacus!

Let's try this. What is 7×5?

$7 \times 5 = 35$. Let's display 35 on the abacus.

Since 35 is already a 2-digit number, we don't need to display zero before 35

$$7 \times 5 = 35$$

1st rod   2nd rod

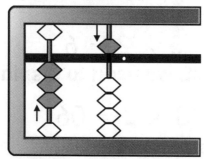

Step 1: Up 3 at 1st rod

Step 2: Up 5 at 2nd rod

Step 3: Equals 35

Try and display these on your abacus.

1 $4 \times 2 = 8$	**2** $5 \times 2 = 10$	**3** $6 \times 2 = 12$
4 $1 \times 3 = 3$	**5** $3 \times 3 = 9$	**6** $7 \times 3 = 21$
7 $6 \times 4 = 24$	**8** $7 \times 4 = 28$	**9** $8 \times 4 = 32$
10 $3 \times 5 = 15$	**11** $6 \times 5 = 30$	**12** $9 \times 5 = 45$

 Let's visualise!

$4 \times 3 =$ ☐

$9 \times 2 =$ ☐

$5 \times 4 =$ ☐

$8 \times 5 =$ ☐

 Visualise the beads for the product of these multiplications.

| 1 $9 \times 2 = 18$ | 2 $2 \times 3 = 6$ | 3 $1 \times 4 = 4$ |
| 4 $5 \times 5 = 25$ | 5 $7 \times 2 = 14$ | 6 $8 \times 3 = 24$ |

Let's solve the following problems!

Devi has 2 eyes. Jenny, Andi, Ah Wai and Zura has 2 eyes too. How many eyes are there altogether?
How many children are there? _5_
How many eyes does each child have? _2_
How many eyes are there altogether?
$5 \times 2 = $ ___

Jenny has 8 tricycles. Each tricycle has 3 wheels. How many wheels are there altogether?
How many tricycles are there? _8_
How many wheels on each tricycle? _3_
How many wheels are there altogether?
$8 \times 3 = $ ___

Andi buys 4 oranges. Ah Wai buys 4 oranges too. How many oranges are there altogether?
How many boys buy the oranges? ___
How many oranges does each boy buy? ___
How many oranges are there altogether?
___ $\times 4 = $ ___

Devi has many beads. She groups the beads into 9 groups. Each group has 5 beads. How many beads does Devi have altogether?
How many groups of beads are there? ___
How many beads in each group? ___
How many beads are there altogether?
___ $\times$ ___ $= $ ___

Let's solve the following problems!

Zura has 24 marbles. She wants to put all her marbles into boxes. She wants 4 marbles in each box. How many boxes does she need?

How many marbles in each box? __4__

How many marbles are there altogether? __24__

How many boxes does she need?

____ × 4 = 24

There are a few jars in the box. Each jar contains 5 cookies. There are 35 cookies altogether. How many jars are there?

How many cookies in each jar? __5__

How many cookies are there altogether? __35__

How many jars are there in the box?

____ × 5 = 35

Jenny has 21 oranges. She wants to give her friends 3 oranges each. How many of her friends will get the oranges?

How many oranges does each friend get? __3__

How many oranges are there altogether? __21__

How many friends will get the oranges?

____ × 3 = 21

Ah Wai eats the same number of eggs every day. In 9 days, he eats 18 eggs. How many eggs does he eat on each day?

How many days does it take him to eat? __9__

How many eggs does he eat altogether? __18__

How many eggs does he eat each day?

9 × ____ = 18

The standard written method!

What is the standard written method for multiplication?

Let's try 3×4. The standard written method is shown below. The product of 3×4 is placed in between the two horizontal lines.

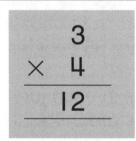

$$
\begin{array}{r}
3 \\
\times\ 4 \\
\hline
12 \\
\hline
\end{array}
$$

Let's write the product of these multiplications following the standard written method.

$\begin{array}{r} 6 \\ \times\ 3 \\ \hline \\ \hline \end{array}$	$\begin{array}{r} 8 \\ \times\ 2 \\ \hline \\ \hline \end{array}$	$\begin{array}{r} 5 \\ \times\ 5 \\ \hline \\ \hline \end{array}$	$\begin{array}{r} 2 \\ \times\ 4 \\ \hline \\ \hline \end{array}$	$\begin{array}{r} 3 \\ \times\ 5 \\ \hline \\ \hline \end{array}$

Write and solve the following according to the standard written method.

1 $3 \times 3 =$ **2** $7 \times 2 =$ **3** $4 \times 5 =$

4 $7 \times 4 =$ **5** $2 \times 5 =$ **6** $9 \times 3 =$

Recall the 2, 3, 4 and 5 times-tables and fill in the blanks with the answers.

1. $3 \times 2 =$ ☐

2. $4 \times 2 =$ ☐

3. $5 \times 2 =$ ☐

4. $4 \times 3 =$ ☐

5. $5 \times 3 =$ ☐

6. $5 \times 4 =$ ☐

7. $2 \times 3 =$ ☐

8. $2 \times 4 =$ ☐

9. $2 \times 5 =$ ☐

10. $3 \times 4 =$ ☐

11. $3 \times 5 =$ ☐

12. $4 \times 5 =$ ☐

Look at your answers again.

Compare your answers on the right column to the answers on the left column.

What do you notice? Discuss with your friends.

Unit 6

Division within
2, 3, 4 and 5 times-tables

Let's try this example differently.

Zura has 24 marbles. She wants to keep all her marbles into boxes. She wants 4 marbles in each box. How many boxes does she need?

Can we solve Zura's problem?

Let's look at the marbles below. There are 24 marbles altogether.

Zura wants 4 marbles in each box. So, let's draw a box that contains 4 marbles. Group the rest of the marbles in fours.

How many boxes have we drawn?
There are 6 boxes altogether.

So, Zura needs 6 boxes to keep all her marbles.
We can write the number sentence this way:

$$24 \div 4 = 6$$

twenty-four divided by four equals six

Recall that $6 \times 4 = 24$

96

With division, we can solve many problems. We can know how to group or share a number of objects equally.

Here are 6 apples.

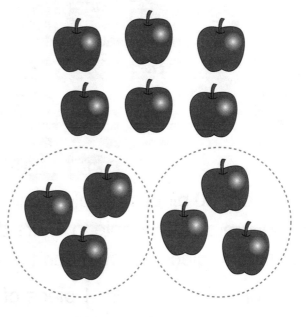

Let's group these apples in threes.

How many groups are there?
There are 2 groups.

We can write the number sentence this way:

$$6 \div 3 = 2$$

six divided by three equals two

Recall that $2 \times 3 = 6$

There are 30 pieces of cakes. Zura wants to share the cakes equally with Devi, Ah Wai, Andi and Jenny. How many pieces should each of them get?

There are 30 pieces of cakes altogether.

There are also 5 people to share the cakes equally.

How many pieces should each of them get?

Let's give each of them 1 piece of cake at a time until all the 30 pieces are given.

Now, let's count how many pieces do each of them get?
Each of them gets 6 pieces.

$$30 \div 5 = 6$$

thirty divided by five equals six

Recall that $6 \times 5 = 30$

From our previous examples,

> $24 \div 4 = 6$; We recalled $6 \times 4 = 24$
>
> $6 \div 3 = 2$; We recalled $2 \times 3 = 6$
>
> $30 \div 5 = 6$; We recalled $6 \times 5 = 30$

We can solve division problems by recalling the number sentences in the times-tables.

Let's look at the 2, 3, 4 and 5 times-tables. Try to solve the division problems.

$1 \times 2 = 2$	$2 \div 2 = \underline{}$	$1 \times 3 = 3$	$3 \div 3 = \underline{}$
$2 \times 2 = 4$	$4 \div 2 = \underline{}$	$2 \times 3 = 6$	$6 \div 3 = \underline{}$
$3 \times 2 = 6$	$6 \div 2 = \underline{}$	$3 \times 3 = 9$	$9 \div 3 = \underline{}$
$4 \times 2 = 8$	$8 \div 2 = \underline{}$	$4 \times 3 = 12$	$12 \div 3 = \underline{}$
$5 \times 2 = 10$	$10 \div 2 = \underline{}$	$5 \times 3 = 15$	$15 \div 3 = \underline{}$
$6 \times 2 = 12$	$12 \div 2 = \underline{}$	$6 \times 3 = 18$	$18 \div 3 = \underline{}$
$7 \times 2 = 14$	$14 \div 2 = \underline{}$	$7 \times 3 = 21$	$21 \div 3 = \underline{}$
$8 \times 2 = 16$	$16 \div 2 = \underline{}$	$8 \times 3 = 24$	$24 \div 3 = \underline{}$
$9 \times 2 = 18$	$18 \div 2 = \underline{}$	$9 \times 3 = 27$	$27 \div 3 = \underline{}$

$1 \times 4 = 4$	$4 \div 4 = \underline{}$	$1 \times 5 = 5$	$5 \div 5 = \underline{}$
$2 \times 4 = 8$	$8 \div 4 = \underline{}$	$2 \times 5 = 10$	$10 \div 5 = \underline{}$
$3 \times 4 = 12$	$12 \div 4 = \underline{}$	$3 \times 5 = 15$	$15 \div 5 = \underline{}$
$4 \times 4 = 16$	$16 \div 4 = \underline{}$	$4 \times 5 = 20$	$20 \div 5 = \underline{}$
$5 \times 4 = 20$	$20 \div 4 = \underline{}$	$5 \times 5 = 25$	$25 \div 5 = \underline{}$
$6 \times 4 = 24$	$24 \div 4 = \underline{}$	$6 \times 5 = 30$	$30 \div 5 = \underline{}$
$7 \times 4 = 28$	$28 \div 4 = \underline{}$	$7 \times 5 = 35$	$35 \div 5 = \underline{}$
$8 \times 4 = 32$	$32 \div 4 = \underline{}$	$8 \times 5 = 40$	$40 \div 5 = \underline{}$
$9 \times 4 = 36$	$36 \div 4 = \underline{}$	$9 \times 5 = 45$	$45 \div 5 = \underline{}$

Let's look at the following problems. Fill in the blanks with the correct answers.

1   Devi has 12 stamps. She gives all her stamps to be shared equally among Andi and Ah Wai. How many stamps does each of the boys get?

What are the numbers involved?

12 stamps and 2 boys

To solve the above problem,
we can write number sentences such as these:

$$12 \div 2 = \bigcirc$$

$$12 = \bigcirc \times 2$$

Each boy will get _____ stamps.

2   Jenny has 40 oranges. She groups the oranges in fives and puts them into a few boxes. If each box contains 5 oranges, how many boxes does she need?

$$40 \div 5 = \bigcirc$$

$$40 = \bigcirc \times 5$$

Jenny needs _____ boxes.

3   Zura has equal number of green, red, blue and black beads. She has 28 beads altogether. How many beads are blue?

$$\bigcirc \div \bigcirc = \bigcirc$$

$$\bigcirc = \bigcirc \times \bigcirc$$

Zura has _____ blue beads.

Let's read these number stories based on the number sentences.

$$36 \div 4 = 9$$

Devi has 36 apples. She can fit the apples into 4 boxes equally. So, there are 9 apples in each box.

$$18 \div 3 = 6$$

Zura has 18 plates. She arranges the same number of plates on 3 shelves. So, there are 6 plates on each shelf.

$$15 \div 5 = 3$$

There are 15 marbles on the table. Jenny groups the marbles in fives. So, there are 3 groups altogether.

Write the number sentences based on their number stories.

Jenny cuts a loaf of bread into 27 slices. She spreads an equal amount of bread slices with strawberry jam, butter and marmalade. So, there are 9 slices of bread with strawberry jam, 9 slices of bread with butter and 9 slices of bread with marmalade.

There are 16 chairs. Ah Wai arranges the same number of chairs in 4 rows. So, there are 4 chairs in each row.

Create your own number stories based on the following number sentences.

❶ $10 \div 2 = 5$	❷ $12 \div 3 = 4$	❸ $32 \div 4 = 8$
❹ $20 \div 4 = 5$	❺ $20 \div 5 = 4$	❻ $24 \div 3 = 8$

Let's look at the following number sentence.

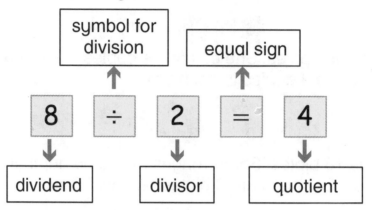

We can write the standard written method for the above division sentence as follows:

$$2 \overline{)\ 8}$$

The above reads 8 divided by 2. There are a few steps that we need to follow to use the standard written method in solving division problems.

Step 1: Divide the dividend by the divisor (8 ÷ 2) and write the answer on top of the dividend as follows:

$$2 \overline{)\ 8}^{\ 4}$$

Step 2: Multiply the answer by the divisor (4 × 2) and write the answer below the dividend (8) as follows:

$$\begin{array}{r} 4 \\ 2 \overline{)\ 8} \\ 8 \end{array}$$

Step 3: Subtract the product from the dividend (8 - 8) as follows:

$$\begin{array}{r} 4 \\ 2 \overline{)\ 8} \\ -8 \\ \hline 0 \end{array}$$

Step 4: The division using the standard written method is complete.

Let's try $45 \div 5$.

$$5 \overline{)\ 45}$$

Step 1: Try to divide the first digit of the dividend by the divisor ($4 \div 5$). 4 is not enough to be divided by 5. So we leave the place on top of 4 blank.

$$5 \overline{)\ 45}$$

Step 2: Use the first and second digit of the dividend together and divide it by the divisor ($45 \div 5$). We know $45 \div 5 = 9$. We write 9 on top of the second digit of the dividend.

$$\begin{array}{r} 9 \\ 5 \overline{)\ 45} \end{array}$$

Step 3: Multiply the answer by the divisor (9×5) and write the answer below the dividend as follows:

$$\begin{array}{r} 9 \\ 5 \overline{)\ 45} \\ 45 \end{array}$$

Step 4: Subtract the product from the dividend ($45 - 45$) as follows:

$$\begin{array}{r} 9 \\ 5 \overline{)\ 45} \\ -\ 45 \\ \hline 0 \end{array}$$

Step 5: The division using the standard written method is complete.

How do we divide 32 by 4 using the abacus?

At this point, we will only learn how to show the dividend, the divisor and the quotient on the abacus.

First, we need to choose the reference point on the abacus. The reference point can be any dot on the beam.

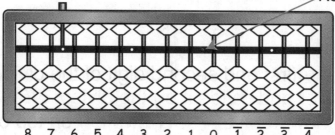

Reference Point

8 7 6 5 4 3 2 1 0 $\overline{1}$ $\overline{2}$ $\overline{3}$ $\overline{4}$

Then, we label the rods as shown above. The first rod on the left of the reference point is labelled 1.

The first rod on the right of the reference point is labelled 0.

The rest of the rods are labelled as shown above. $\overline{1}$, $\overline{2}$, $\overline{3}$ and $\overline{4}$ are called bar 1, bar 2, bar 3 and bar 4 respectively.

After labelling the rods, we need to know where we should place the dividend, the divisor and the quotient.

Let's try 32 ÷ 4. Where do we place the dividend?

To place the dividend, we need to look at the following formula:

$$m - n - 1$$
where
m : Number of digits for dividend
n : Number of digits for divisor

$\boxed{32}$ $\boxed{\div}$ $\boxed{4}$ $\boxed{=}$ $\boxed{?}$

The dividend, 32 has 2 digits (m). The divisor, 4 has 1 digit (n). According to the formula,

$$m - n - 1 = ?$$
$$2 - 1 - 1 = 0.$$

So, we start placing the dividend at the rod labelled 0. To Up 32,

Up 3 at 0, Up 2 at rod $\overline{1}$

Dividend

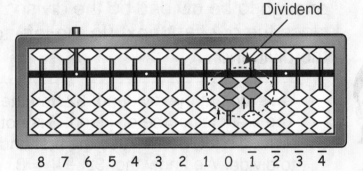

8 7 6 5 4 3 2 1 0 $\overline{1}$ $\overline{2}$ $\overline{3}$ $\overline{4}$

Where do we place the divisor?

We place the divisor, 4 at the first rod from the left frame of the abacus.

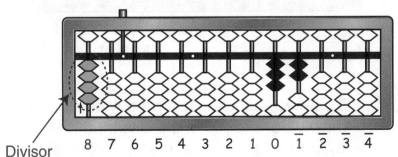

Divisor

8 7 6 5 4 3 2 1 0 $\overline{1}$ $\overline{2}$ $\overline{3}$ $\overline{4}$

Where do we place the quotient?

The placement of the quotient depends on the dividend.

If the first digit of the dividend is enough to be divided by the divisor, we start placing the quotient by skipping one rod to the left of the dividend.

If the first digit of the dividend is not enough to be divided by the divisor, we place the quotient next (to the left) to the dividend.

Let's look at the dividend, 32 and the divisor, 4. The first digit of the dividend, 3 is not enough to be divided by 4. So, we use the first and second digit to divide. We know that $32 \div 4 = 8$.

We place the quotient, 8 next to the dividend.

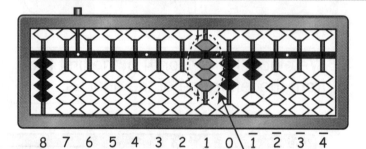

8 7 6 5 4 3 2 1 0 $\bar{1}$ $\bar{2}$ $\bar{3}$ $\bar{4}$

Quotient

Are we done?

For now, we'll just stop here. We now know where to place the dividend, the divisor and the quotient on the abacus!

Step 1: Choose a reference point and label the rods.

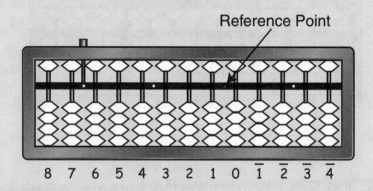

Reference Point

8 7 6 5 4 3 2 1 0 $\bar{1}$ $\bar{2}$ $\bar{3}$ $\bar{4}$

Step 2: Determine the placement of the dividend.
According to the formula, m − n − 1:

Number of digits for the dividend, $9 = 1$
Number of digits for the divisor, $3 = 1$

$$m - n - 1 = ?$$
$$1 - 1 - 1 = -1 \text{ or } \bar{1}$$

So, up 9 at $\bar{1}$.

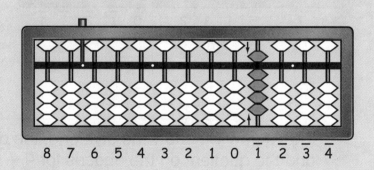

8 7 6 5 4 3 2 1 0 $\bar{1}$ $\bar{2}$ $\bar{3}$ $\bar{4}$

Step 3: Place the divisor at the first rod from the left of the abacus.

So, up 3 at rod 8.

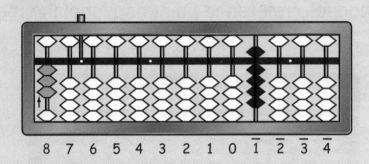

$$8\ 7\ 6\ 5\ 4\ 3\ 2\ 1\ 0\ \overline{1}\ \overline{2}\ \overline{3}\ \overline{4}$$

Step 4: Since 9 is enough to divide by 3, we skip one rod to the left and place the quotient there.

$$9 \div 3 = 3$$

So, up 3 at rod 1.

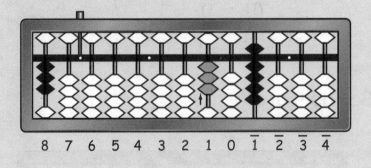

$$8\ 7\ 6\ 5\ 4\ 3\ 2\ 1\ 0\ \overline{1}\ \overline{2}\ \overline{3}\ \overline{4}$$

That's how we show the dividend, the divisor and the quotient on the abacus for $9 \div 3 = 3$.

Fill in the blanks with the right answers. Then, show the dividend, the divisor and the quotient on the abacus.

2 ÷ 2 =	4 ÷ 2 =	6 ÷ 2 =
3 ÷ 3 =	6 ÷ 3 =	9 ÷ 3 =
4 ÷ 4 =	8 ÷ 4 =	12 ÷ 4 =
5 ÷ 5 =	10 ÷ 5 =	15 ÷ 5 =
8 ÷ 2 =	10 ÷ 2 =	12 ÷ 2 =
12 ÷ 3 =	15 ÷ 3 =	18 ÷ 3 =
16 ÷ 4 =	20 ÷ 4 =	24 ÷ 4 =
20 ÷ 5 =	25 ÷ 5 =	30 ÷ 5 =
14 ÷ 2 =	16 ÷ 2 =	18 ÷ 2 =
21 ÷ 3 =	24 ÷ 3 =	27 ÷ 3 =
28 ÷ 4 =	32 ÷ 4 =	36 ÷ 4 =
35 ÷ 5 =	40 ÷ 5 =	45 ÷ 5 =

Learn these by heart!

1 × 2 = 2	2 ÷ 2 = 1
2 × 2 = 4	4 ÷ 2 = 2
3 × 2 = 6	6 ÷ 2 = 3
4 × 2 = 8	8 ÷ 2 = 4
5 × 2 = 10	10 ÷ 2 = 5
6 × 2 = 12	12 ÷ 2 = 6
7 × 2 = 14	14 ÷ 2 = 7
8 × 2 = 16	16 ÷ 2 = 8
9 × 2 = 18	18 ÷ 2 = 9

1 × 3 = 3	3 ÷ 3 = 1
2 × 3 = 6	6 ÷ 3 = 2
3 × 3 = 9	9 ÷ 3 = 3
4 × 3 = 12	12 ÷ 3 = 4
5 × 3 = 15	15 ÷ 3 = 5
6 × 3 = 18	18 ÷ 3 = 6
7 × 3 = 21	21 ÷ 3 = 7
8 × 3 = 24	24 ÷ 3 = 8
9 × 3 = 27	27 ÷ 3 = 9

1 × 4 = 4	4 ÷ 4 = 1
2 × 4 = 8	8 ÷ 4 = 2
3 × 4 = 12	12 ÷ 4 = 3
4 × 4 = 16	16 ÷ 4 = 4
5 × 4 = 20	20 ÷ 4 = 5
6 × 4 = 24	24 ÷ 4 = 6
7 × 4 = 28	28 ÷ 4 = 7
8 × 4 = 32	32 ÷ 4 = 8
9 × 4 = 36	36 ÷ 4 = 9

1 × 5 = 5	5 ÷ 5 = 1
2 × 5 = 10	10 ÷ 5 = 2
3 × 5 = 15	15 ÷ 5 = 3
4 × 5 = 20	20 ÷ 5 = 4
5 × 5 = 25	25 ÷ 5 = 5
6 × 5 = 30	30 ÷ 5 = 6
7 × 5 = 35	35 ÷ 5 = 7
8 × 5 = 40	40 ÷ 5 = 8
9 × 5 = 45	45 ÷ 5 = 9